Tropical Fish
Charted Designs

Barbara Christopher

Dover Publications, Inc.
New York

To Pastor Larry Pitta and Mrs. Margie Pitta
of Christ-to-the-Community Church,
Bay Ridge, Brooklyn, with affection

Copyright © 1992 by Dover Publications, Inc.
All rights reserved under Pan American and International Copyright Conventions.

Published in Canada by General Publishing Company, Ltd., 30 Lesmill Road, Don Mills, Toronto, Ontario.
Published in the United Kingdom by Constable and Company, Ltd., 3 The Lanchesters, 162–164 Fulham Palace Road, London W6 9ER.

Tropical Fish Charted Designs is a new work, first published by Dover Publications, Inc., in 1992.

Manufactured in the United States of America
Dover Publications, Inc., 31 East 2nd Street, Mineola, N.Y. 11501

Library of Congress Cataloging-in-Publication Data

Christopher, Barbara.
    Tropical fish charted designs / Barbara Christopher.
        p.   cm. — (Dover needlework series)
    ISBN 0-486-27341-5
    1. Embroidery—Patterns.   2. Fishes in art.   I. Title.   II. Series.
TT773.C56   1992
746.44'041—dc20   92-24968
                                                                        CIP

Introduction

The keeping of tropical fish is an extremely popular hobby, and it is easy to understand why when you see the dazzling array of designs presented in this new collection by Barbara Christopher. One hundred different types of fish are depicted in the 87 designs featured here, including such exotic species as the Siamese Fighting Fish, the Moorish Idol, the Regal Angelfish and several different types of goldfish. A variety of styles and sizes is included, from tiny spot motifs, to borders, to full-page scenes featuring many different fish.

The fascinating shapes and the gorgeous colors of these jewels of the sea make this group of designs particularly appealing. Many include suggestions for using metallic threads to more accurately capture their iridescent quality.

These designs were originally created for counted cross-stitch, but they are easily translated into other needlework techniques. Keep in mind that the finished piece will not be the same size as the charted design unless you are working on fabric or canvas with the same number of threads per inch as the chart has squares per inch. With knitting and crocheting, the size will vary according to the number of stitches per inch.

COUNTED CROSS-STITCH

MATERIALS

1. **Needles.** A small blunt tapestry needle, No. 24 or No. 26.

2. **Fabric.** Evenweave linen, cotton, wool or synthetic fabrics all work well. The most popular fabrics are aida cloth, linen and hardanger cloth. Cotton aida is most commonly available in 18 threads-per-inch, 14 threads-per-inch and 11 threads-per-inch (14-count is the most popular size). Evenweave linen comes in a variety of threads-per-inch. To work cross-stitch on linen involves a slightly different technique (see page 4). Thirty thread-per-inch linen will result in a stitch about the same size as 14-count aida. Hardanger cloth has 22 threads to the inch and is available in cotton or linen. The amount of fabric needed depends on the size of the cross-stitch design. To determine yardage, divide the number of stitches in the design by the thread-count of the fabric. For example: If a design 112 squares wide by 140 squares deep is worked on a 14-count fabric, divide 112 by 14 (=8), and 140 by 14 (=10). The design will measure 8″ × 10″. The same design worked on 22-count fabric measures about 5″ × 6½″. When cutting the fabric, be sure to allow at least 2″ of blank fabric all around the design for finishing.

3. **Threads and Yarns.** Six-strand embroidery floss, crewel wool, pearl cotton or metallic threads all work well for cross-stitch. DMC Embroidery Floss and Balger Metallic Yarn* have been used to color-code the patterns in this volume.

4. **Embroidery Hoop.** A wooden or plastic 4″, 5″ or 6″ round or oval hoop with a screw-type tension adjuster works best for cross-stitch.

5. **Scissors.** A pair of sharp embroidery scissors is essential to all embroidery.

PREPARING TO WORK

To prevent raveling, either whip stitch or machine-stitch the outer edges of the fabric.

Locate the exact center of the chart. Establish the center of the fabric by folding it in half first vertically, then horizontally. The center stitch of the chart falls where the creases of the fabric meet. Mark the fabric center with a basting thread.

It is best to begin cross-stitch at the top of the design. To establish the top, count the squares up from the center of the chart, and the corresponding number of holes up from the center of the fabric.

Place the fabric tautly in the embroidery hoop, for tension makes it easier to push the needle through the holes without piercing the fibers. While working continue to retighten the fabric as necessary.

When working with multiple strands (such as embroidery floss) always separate (strand) the thread before beginning to stitch. This one small step allows for better coverage of the fabric. When you need more than one thread in the needle, use separate strands and do not double the thread. (For example: If you need four strands, use four separated strands.) Thread has a nap (just as fabrics do) and can be felt to be smoother in one direction than the other. Always work with the nap (the smooth side) pointing down.

For 14-count aida and 30-count linen, work with two strands of six-strand floss. For more texture, use more thread; for a flatter look, use less thread.

---

*For information on where to obtain Balger Metallic Yarn write to Kreinik Manufacturing Co., Inc., Dept. D2, P.O. Box 1966, Parkersburg, West Virginia 26102.

EMBROIDERY

To begin, fasten the thread with a waste knot and hold a short length of thread on the underside of the work, anchoring it with the first few stitches (*Diagram 1*). When the thread end is securely in place, clip the knot.

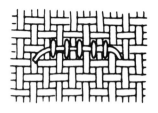

DIAGRAM 1
Reverse side of work

To stitch, push the needle up through a hole in the fabric, cross the thread intersection (or square) on a left-to-right diagonal (*Diagram 2*). Half the stitch is now completed.

Next, cross back, right to left, forming an X (*Diagram 3*).

DIAGRAM 2

Work all the same color stitches on one row, then cross back, completing the X's (*Diagram 4*).

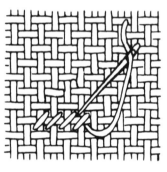 

DIAGRAM 3   **DIAGRAM 4**

Some needleworkers prefer to cross each stitch as they come to it. This method also works, but be sure all of the top stitches are slanted in the same direction. Isolated stitches must be crossed as they are worked. Vertical stitches are crossed as shown in *Diagram 5*.

DIAGRAM 5

At the top, work horizontal rows of a single color, left to right. This method allows you to go from an unoccupied space to an occupied space (working from an empty hole to a filled one), making ruffling of the floss less likely. Holes are used more than once, and all stitches "hold hands" unless a space is indicated on the chart. Hold the work upright throughout (do not turn as with many needlepoint stitches).

When carrying the thread from one area to another, run the needle under a few stitches on the wrong side. Do not carry the thread across an open expanse of fabric as it will be visible from the front when the project is completed.

To end a color, weave in and out of the underside of the stitches, making a scallop stitch or two for extra security (*Diagram 6*). When possible, end in the same direction in which you were working, jumping up a row if necessary (*Diagram 7*). This prevents holes caused by stitches being pulled in two directions. Trim the thread ends closely and do not leave any tails or knots as they will show through the fabric when the work is completed.

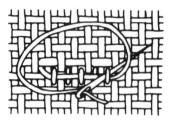

DIAGRAM 6
Reverse side of work

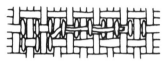

DIAGRAM 7
Reverse side of work

A number of other counted-thread stitches can be used in cross-stitch. Backstitch (*Diagram 8*) is used for outlines, face details and the like. It is worked from hole to hole, and may be stitched as a vertical, horizontal or diagonal line.

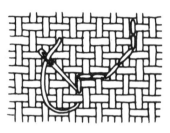

DIAGRAM 8

Straight stitch is worked from side to side over several threads (*Diagram 9*) and affords solid coverage.

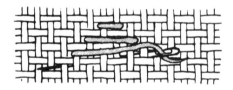

DIAGRAM 9

French knots (*Diagram 10*) are handy for special effects. They are worked in the same manner as on regular embroidery.

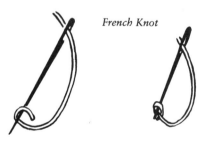

French Knot

DIAGRAM 10

Embroidery on Linen. Working on linen requires a slightly different technique. While evenweave linen is remarkably regular, there are always a few thick or thin threads. To keep the stitches even, cross-stitch is worked over two threads in each direction (*Diagram 11*).

DIAGRAM 11

As you are working over more threads, linen affords a greater variation in stitches. A half-stitch can slant in either direction and is uncrossed. A three-quarters stitch is shown in *Diagram 12*.

DIAGRAM 12

Diagram 13 shows the backstitch worked on linen.

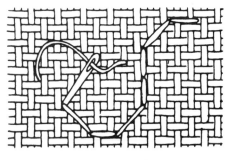

DIAGRAM 13

Embroidery on Gingham. Gingham and other checked fabrics can be used for cross-stitch. Using the fabric as a guide, work the stitches from corner to corner of each check.

Embroidery on Uneven-Weave Fabrics. If you wish to work cross-stitch on an uneven-weave fabric, baste a lightweight Penelope needlepoint canvas to the material. The design can then be stitched by working the cross-stitch over the double mesh of the canvas. When working in this manner, take care not to catch the threads of the canvas in the embroidery. After the cross-stitch is completed, remove the basting threads. With tweezers remove first the vertical threads, one strand at a time, of the needlepoint canvas, then the horizontal threads.

NEEDLEPOINT

One of the most common methods for working needlepoint is from a charted design. By simply viewing each square of a chart as a stitch on the canvas, the patterns quickly and easily translate from one technique to another.

MATERIALS

1. **Needles.** A blunt tapestry needle with a rounded tip and an elongated eye. The needle must clear the hole of the canvas without spreading the threads. For No. 10 canvas, a No. 18 needle works best.

2. **Canvas.** There are two distinct types of needlepoint canvas: single-mesh (mono canvas) and double-mesh (Penelope canvas). Single-mesh canvas, the more common of the two, is easier on the eyes as the spaces are slightly larger. Double-mesh canvas has two horizontal and two vertical threads forming each mesh. The latter is a very stable canvas on which the threads stay securely in place as the work progresses. Canvas is available in many sizes, from 5 mesh-per-inch to 18 mesh-per-inch, and even smaller. The number of mesh-per-inch will, of course, determine the dimensions of the finished needlepoint project. A 60 square × 120 square chart will measure 12″ × 24″ on 5 mesh-to-the-inch canvas, 5″ × 10″ on 12 mesh-to-the-inch canvas. The most common canvas size is 10 to the inch.

3. **Yarns.** Persian, crewel and tapestry yarns all work well on needlepoint canvas.

PREPARING TO WORK

Allow 1″ to 1½″ blank canvas all around. Bind the raw edges of the canvas with masking tape or machine-stitched double-fold bias tape.

There are few hard-and-fast rules on where to begin the design. It is best to complete the main motif, then fill in the background as the last step.

For any guidelines you wish to draw on the canvas, take care that your marking medium is waterproof. Nonsoluble ink, acrylic paints thinned with water so as not to clog the mesh, and waterproof felt-tip pens all work well. If unsure, experiment on a scrap of canvas.

When working with multiple strands (such as Persian yarn) always separate (strand) the yarn before beginning to stitch. This one small step allows for better coverage of the canvas. When you need more than one piece of yarn in the needle, use separate strands and do not double the yarn. For example: If you need two strands of 3-ply Persian yarn, use two separated strands. Yarn has a nap (just as fabrics do) and can be felt to be smoother in one direction than the other. Always work with the nap (the smooth side) pointing down.

For 5 mesh-to-the-inch canvas, use six strands of 3-ply yarn; for 10 mesh-to-the-inch canvas, use three strands of 3-ply yarn.

STITCHING

Cut yarn lengths 18″ long. Begin needlepoint by holding about 1″ of loose yarn on the wrong side of the work and working the first several stitches over the loose end to secure it. To end a piece of yarn, run it under several completed stitches on the wrong side of the work.

There are hundreds of needlepoint stitch variations, but tent stitch is universally considered to be *the* needlepoint stitch. The most familiar versions of tent stitch are half-cross stitch, continental stitch and basket-weave stitch.

Half-cross stitch (*Diagram 14*) is worked from left to right. The canvas is then turned around and the return row is again stitched from left to right. Holding the needle vertically, bring it to the front of the canvas

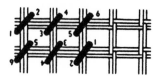

DIAGRAM 14

through the hole that will be the bottom of the first stitch. Keep the stitches loose for minimum distortion and good coverage. Half-cross stitch is best worked on a double-mesh canvas.

Continental stitch (*Diagram 15*) begins in the upper right-hand corner and is worked from right to left. The needle is slanted and always brought out a mesh ahead. The resulting stitch appears as a half-cross stitch on the front and as a slanting stitch on the back. When the row is complete, turn the canvas around to work the return row, continuing to stitch from right to left.

DIAGRAM 15

Basket-weave stitch (*Diagram 16*) begins in the upper right-hand corner with four continental stitches (two stitches worked horizontally across the top and two placed directly below the first stitch). Work diagonal rows, the first slanting up and across the canvas from right to left, and the next down and across from left to right. Moving down the canvas from left to right, the needle is in a vertical position; working in the opposite direction, the needle is horizontal.

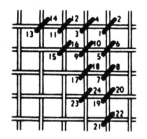

DIAGRAM 16

The rows interlock, creating a basket-weave pattern on the wrong side. If the stitch is not done properly, a faint ridge will show where the pattern was interrupted. On basket-weave stitch, always stop working in the middle of a row, rather than at the end, so that you will know in which direction you were working.

KNITTING

Charted designs can be worked into stockinette stitch as you are knitting, or they can be embroidered with duplicate stitch when the knitting is complete. For the former, wind the different colors of yarn on bobbins and work in the same manner as in Fair Isle knitting. A few quick Fair Isle tips: (1) Always bring up the new color yarn from under the dropped color to prevent holes. (2) Carry the color not in use loosely across the wrong side of the work, but not more than three or four stitches without twisting the yarns. If a color is not in use for more than seven or eight stitches, it is usually best to drop that color yarn and rejoin a new bobbin when the color is again needed.

CROCHET

There are a number of ways in which charts can be used for crochet. Among them are:

SINGLE CROCHET

Single crochet is often seen worked in multiple colors. When changing colors, always pick up the new color for the last yarn-over of the old color. The color not in use can be carried loosely across the back of the work for a few stitches, or you can work the single crochet over the unused color. The latter method makes for a neater appearance on the wrong side, but sometimes the old color peeks through the stitches. This method can also be applied to half-double crochet and double crochet, but keep in mind that the longer stitches will distort the design.

FILET CROCHET

This technique is nearly always worked from charts and uses only one color thread. The result is a solid-color piece with the design filled in and the background left as an open mesh. Care must be taken in selecting the design, as the longer stitch causes distortion.

AFGHAN CROCHET

The most common method here is cross-stitch worked over the afghan stitch. Complete the afghan crochet project. Then, following the chart for color placement, work cross-stitch over the squares of crochet.

OTHER CHARTED METHODS

Latch hook, Assisi embroidery, beading, cross-stitch on needlepoint canvas (a European favorite) and lace net embroidery are among the other needlework methods worked from charts.

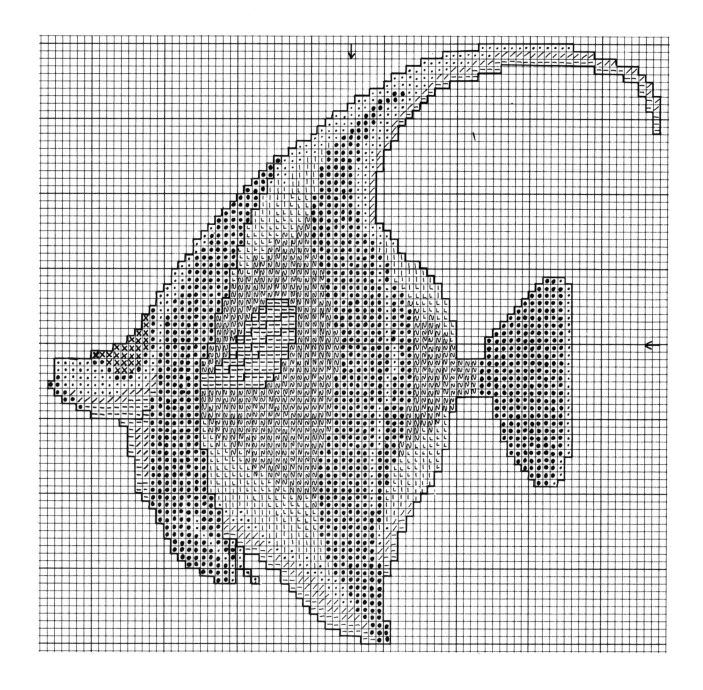

Moorish Idol
Zanclus canescens

85 stitches by 80 stitches

BACK-STITCH	CROSS-STITCH	DMC #	
	⊡		white
——	⊙	310	black
	⊟	318	light steel gray
	☒	740	tangerine
	ﺉ	743	dark yellow
	⌊	744	medium yellow
	⌶	745	light yellow
	⧄	762	very light pearl gray

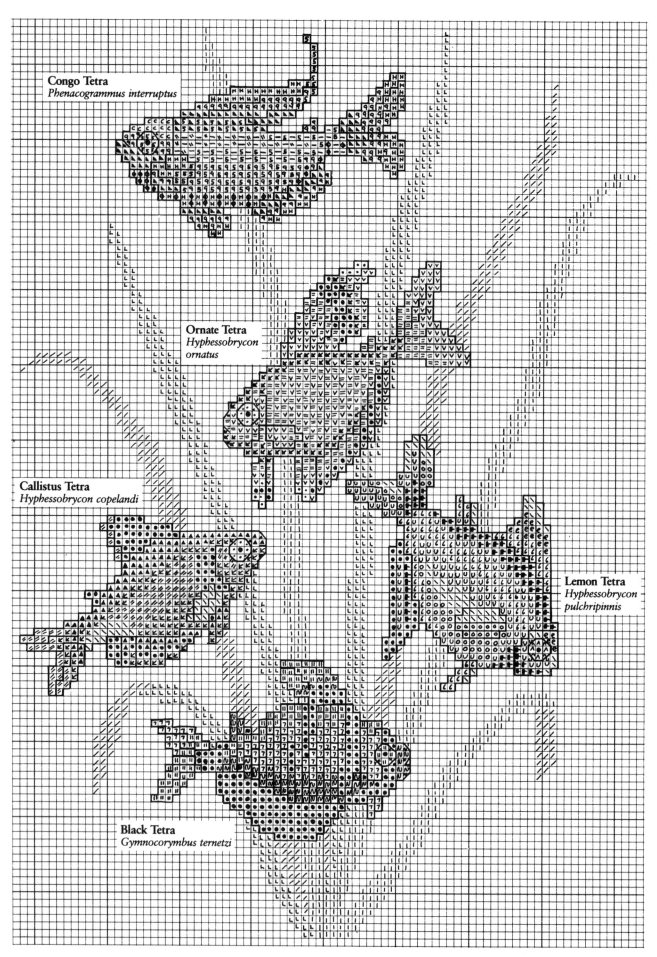

Congo Tetra
Phenacogrammus interruptus

Ornate Tetra
Hyphessobrycon ornatus

Callistus Tetra
Hyphessobrycon copelandi

Lemon Tetra
Hyphessobrycon pulchripinnis

Black Tetra
Gymnocorymbus ternetzi

◄ Tetras

85 stitches by 121 stitches

BACK-STITCH	CROSS-STITCH	DMC #	
	·		white
—	●	310	black
	Ⅲ	317	pewter gray
	⊿	318	light steel gray
	◣	340	medium lilac
	◪	341	light lilac
	▲	349	dark coral
	⊠	350	medium coral
	⧄	351	coral
	⊖	402	very light mahogany
	⋈	413	dark pewter gray
	⫿	471	light avocado green
	⧄	472	very light avocado green
	⌀	598	light turquoise
	Λ	606	bright orange red
	⊍	725	topaz
	◻	742	light tangerine
	◨	743	dark yellow
	5	747	very light sky blue
	⊟	772	very light golden green
	⊞	783	Christmas gold
	⌴	907	light parrot green
	⧆	927	light gray blue
	⊞	928	very light gray blue
	⊠	955	light Nile green
	◪	3685	dark mauve
	⊟	3687	mauve
	⋁	3688	medium light mauve
	⊂	3689	light mauve

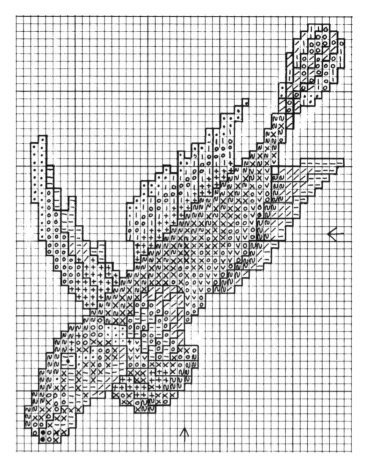

▲ Dragonet

Callionymus lyra

44 stitches by 56 stitches

FRENCH KNOT	BACK-STITCH	CROSS-STITCH	DMC #	
·	—	●	300	very dark mahogany
		⊠	517	dark Wedgwood blue
		⊻	518	light Wedgwood blue
		⫿	519	sky blue
		⊙	725	topaz
		·	726	light topaz
		⊟	747	very light sky blue
		⧄	772	very light loden green
		⊞	783	Christmas gold
		⋈	921	copper

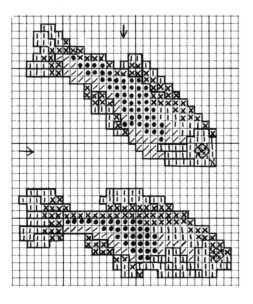

◄ Harlequin Rasbora

Rasbora heteromorpha

29 stitches by 34 stitches

BACK-STITCH	CROSS-STITCH	DMC #	
—	●	310	black
	⧄	353	peach
	⊠	3340	melon
	⫿	3341	light melon

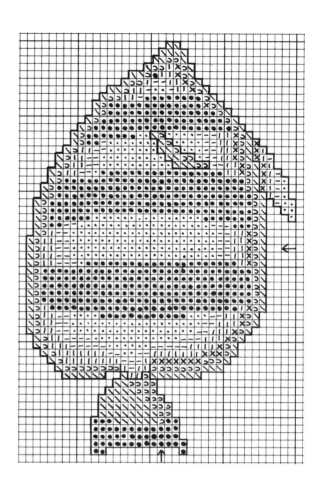

▼ **Regal Angelfish**
Pygoplites diacanthus
57 stitches by 45 stitches

BACK-STITCH	CROSS-STITCH	DMC #	
	·		white
	●	310	black
	ℵ	318	light steel gray
	Ʊ	415	pearl gray
	Y	741	medium tangerine
	I	742	light tangerine
	/	743	dark yellow
	‖	772	very light loden green
	▼	798	dark Delft blue
⁓⁓⁓	✕	996	medium electric blue
	◨	3364	light loden green

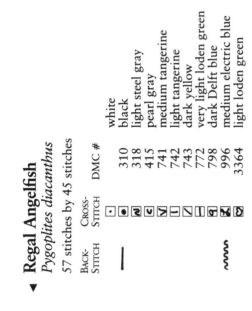

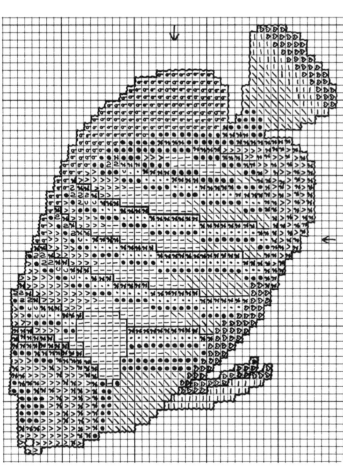

Lord Howe Butterflyfish ▶
Chaetodon tricinctus
55 stitches by 37 stitches

BACK-STITCH	CROSS-STITCH	DMC #	
	·		white
	●	310	black
	✕	414	dark steel gray
	I	415	pearl gray
	⊡	762	very light pearl gray
	Ʊ	947	burnt orange
	◿	970	light pumpkin

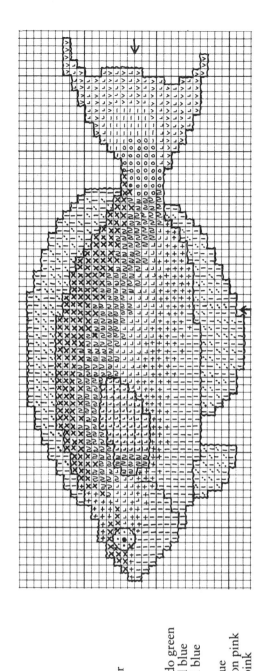

▼ **Undulate Triggerfish**
Balistapus undulatus

58 stitches by 37 stitches

BACK-STITCH	CROSS-STITCH	DMC #	
	⊡		white
～～	◣	413	dark pewter gray
	◩	676	light old gold
	S	680	dark old gold
	○	729	medium old gold
---	I	3078	very light golden yellow
	☒	3346	hunter green
	L	3347	medium yellow green

Splendid Perch ▶
Callanthias allporti

72 stitches by 30 stitches

BACK-STITCH	CROSS-STITCH	DMC #	
	·		white
	L	210	medium lavender
	○	307	lemon yellow
	○	310	black
	⊞	341	light lilac
	I	472	very light avocado green
	V	517	dark Wedgwood blue
～～	I	518	light Wedgwood blue
	⸫	519	sky blue
---	☒	747	very light sky blue
	N	892	medium carnation pink
		893	light carnation pink

11

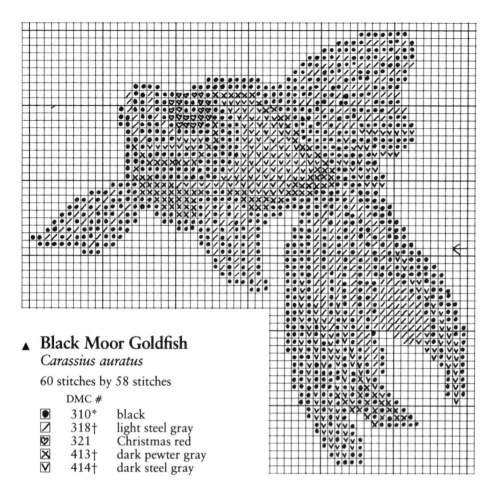

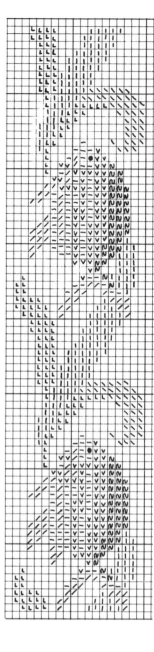

▲ Black Moor Goldfish
Carassius auratus

60 stitches by 58 stitches

	DMC #	
◕	310*	black
⁄	318†	light steel gray
♥	321	Christmas red
✕	413†	dark pewter gray
ⱽ	414†	dark steel gray

*Use 1 strand of Balger Blending Filament #005HL high
 luster black with this color
†Use 1 strand of Balger Blending Filament #010HL high
 luster steel gray with these colors

▼ Glowlight Tetra Border
Hemigrammus erythrozonus

38-stitch repeat by 22 stitches

BACK-STITCH	CROSS-STITCH	DMC #		BACK-STITCH	CROSS-STITCH	DMC #	
—	◕	310	black		⊙	415*	pearl gray
	⁄	318*	light steel gray		✕	608	bright orange
∿∿		413	dark pewter gray		⊡	762*	very light pearl gray
	⏐	414*	dark steel gray				

*Use 1 strand of Balger Blending Filament #032 pearl with each of these colors

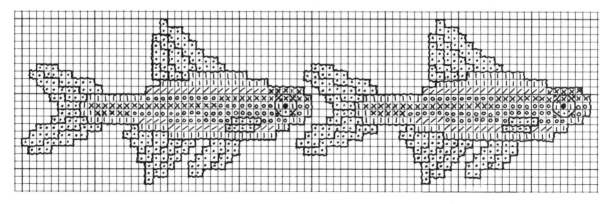

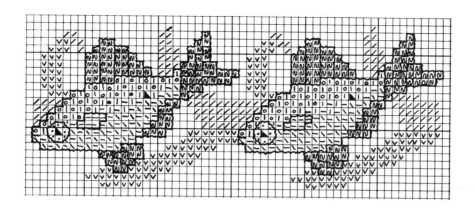

◄ Egg-fish (Goldfish) Border
Carassius auratus

18 stitches by 39-stitch repeat

	DMC #	
◉	310	black
◩	472	very light avocado green
ℕ	606	bright orange red
☑	608	bright orange
◫	704	bright chartreuse
⊟	740	tangerine
◪	742	light tangerine
◱	907	light parrot green

▲ Rosy Barb Border
Barbus conchonius

28-stitch repeat by 22 stitches

Back-Stitch	Cross-Stitch	DMC #	
	⊡		white
	☑	702	kelly green
	◪	704	bright chartreuse
	◩	818	baby pink
∼∼	◼	902	very dark garnet red
	ℕ	3685	dark mauve
	◉	3687	mauve
	⊟	3688	medium light mauve
	◫	3689	light mauve

▼ Swordtail
Xiphophorus helleri

63 stitches by 26 stitches

Back-Stitch	Cross-Stitch	DMC #	
	⊡		white
	◉	310	black
—	☒	349*	dark coral
	◫	351*	coral
	◪	415	pearl gray

*Use 1 strand of Balger Blending Filament #003 HL
high luster red with these colors

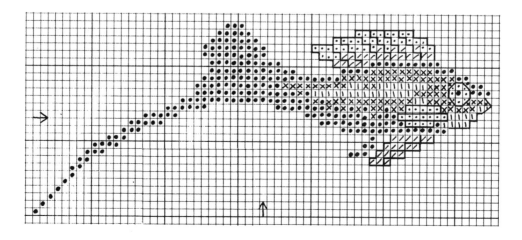

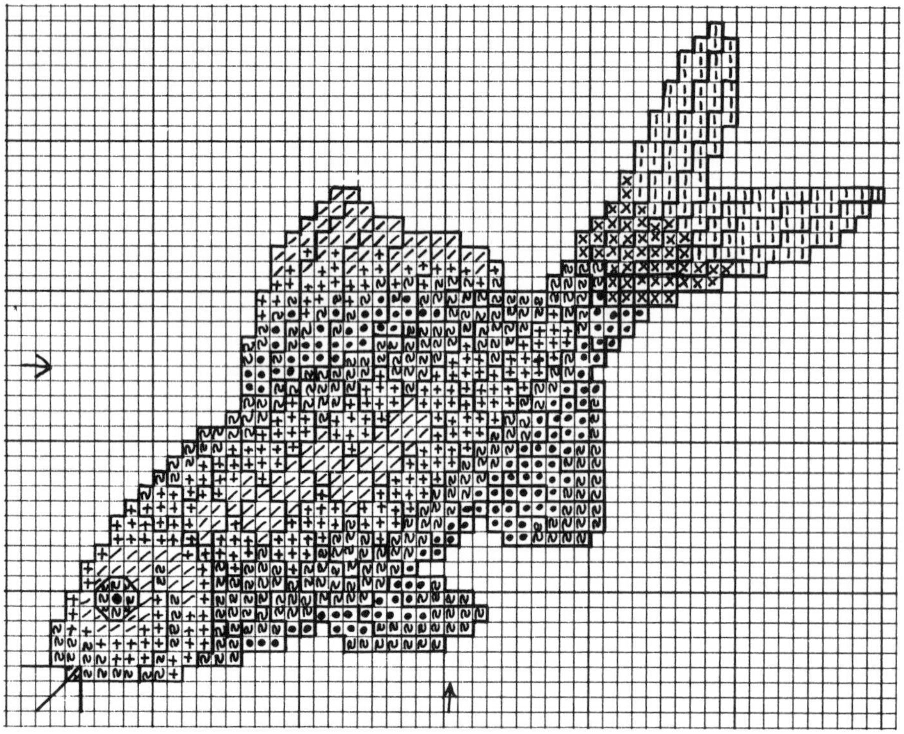

▲ **Red-tailed Black "Shark"**

Labeo bicolor

59 stitches by 46 stitches

Back-Stitch	Cross-Stitch	DMC #	
—	●	310	black
	N	550*	very dark violet
	X	606†	bright orange red
	I	608†	bright orange
	+	3685*	dark mauve
	/	3687*	mauve

*Use 1 strand of Balger Blending Filament #024 fuchsia with these colors

†Use 1 strand of Balger Blending Filament #003 red with these colors

▼ **Lionhead Goldfish**

Carassius auratus

66 stitches by 34 stitches

Back-Stitch	Cross-Stitch	DMC #	
	·		white
—	●	310	black
~~		612	medium drab brown
	L	740	tangerine
	/	742	light tangerine
	I	744	medium yellow
	X	947	burnt orange

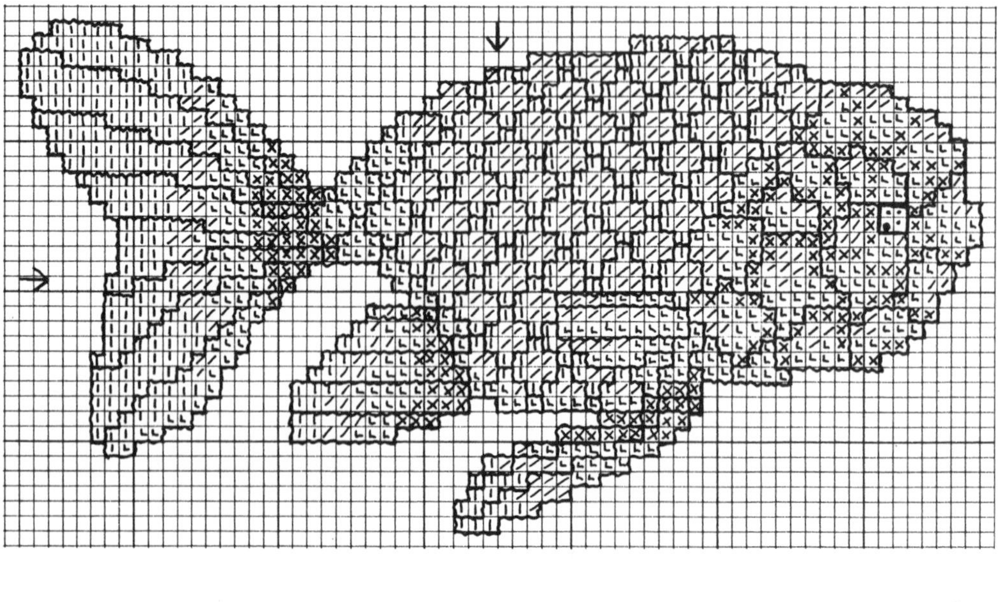

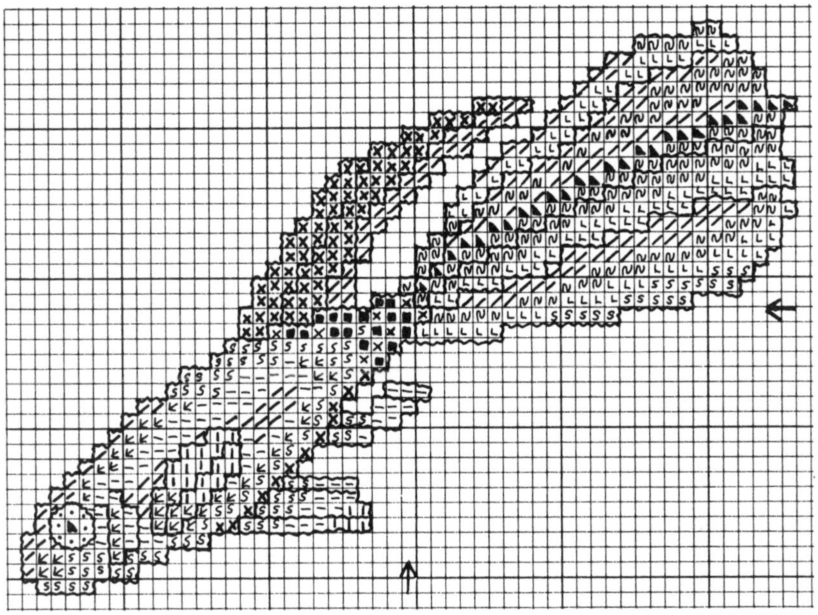

▲ **Veil-tail Guppy**

Poecilia reticulata

53 stitches by 38 stitches

Back-Stitch	Cross-Stitch	DMC #	
	•		white
	K	740	tangerine
	–	742	light tangerine
	I	743	dark yellow
	/	813	light blue
~~	◣	824	very dark blue
	N	825	dark blue
	L	826	medium blue
	X	900	dark burnt orange
	S	947	burnt orange
	■	991	dark aquamarine
	II	992	aquamarine

▼ **Chinese Algae Eater**

Gyrinocheilus aymonieri

62 stitches by 42 stitches

Back-Stitch	Cross-Stitch	DMC #	
—	●	310	black
	I	744	medium yellow
	•	745	light yellow
	–	772	very light loden green
	U	906	medium parrot green
	V	907	light parrot green
	9	913	medium Nile green
	/	955	light Nile green
	L	3013	light khaki green
	X	3363	loden green
	\	3364	light loden green

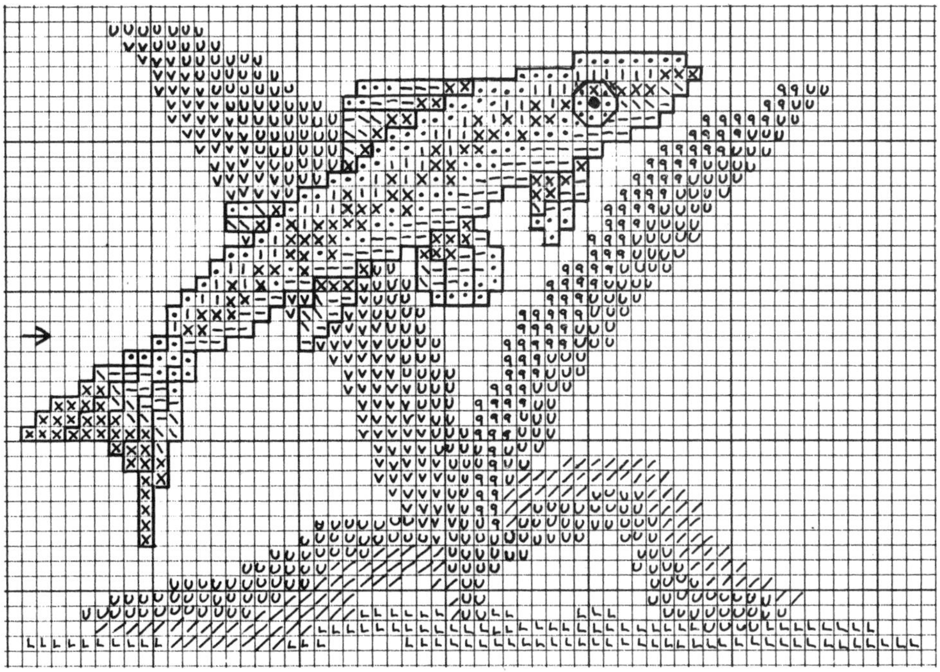

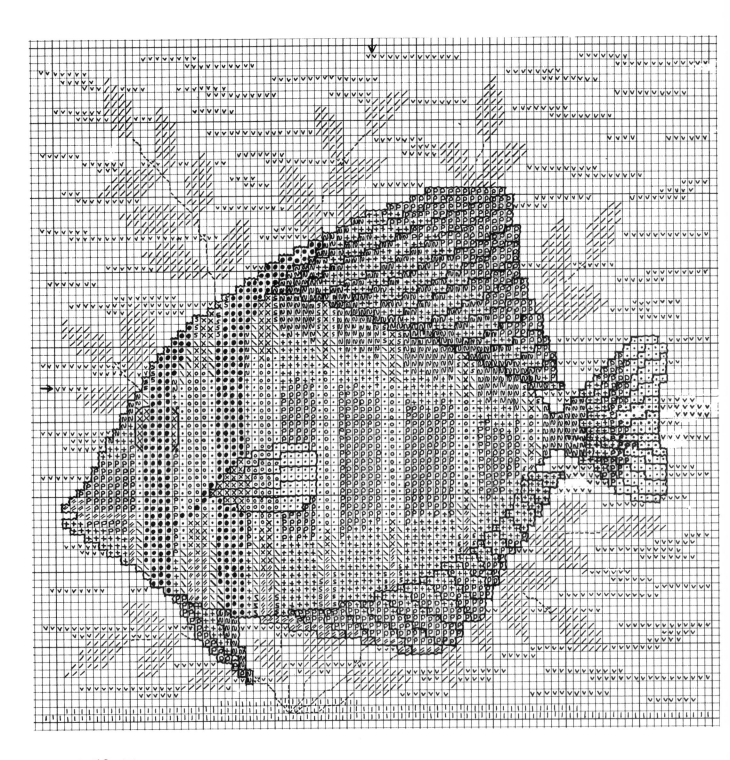

Sailfin Tang
Zebrasoma veliferum

92 stitches by 89 stitches

BACK-STITCH	CROSS-STITCH	DMC #	
	·		white
—	●	310	black
		469	avocado green
ᶰᶰᶰ	И	470	medium light avocado green
	⊞	471	light avocado green
	P	472	very light avocado green
	V	519	sky blue
	⁄⁄	742	light tangerine

BACK-STITCH	CROSS-STITCH	DMC #	
	⊠	743	dark yellow
	⊙	744	medium yellow
- - -		913	medium Nile green
	⁄	955	light Nile green
	S	3023	light brown gray
	И	3024	very light brown gray
	⊓	3033	very light mocha brown

Polkadot Cardinalfish
Sphaeramia nematopterus

91 stitches by 68 stitches

BACK-Stitch	CROSS-Stitch	DMC #	
	⊡		white
	V̄	307	lemon yellow
	●	407	dark cocoa brown
	⊟	444	dark lemon yellow
	⊠	445	light lemon yellow
∿	▼	451	dark shell gray
	V	452	medium shell gray
	L	725	topaz
	o	740	tangerine
	⊿	741	medium tangerine
	ℕ	780	very dark topaz
	S	783	Christmas gold
	Z	869	very dark hazelnut brown
	+	954	Nile green
	E	976	medium golden brown
	X	977	light golden brown

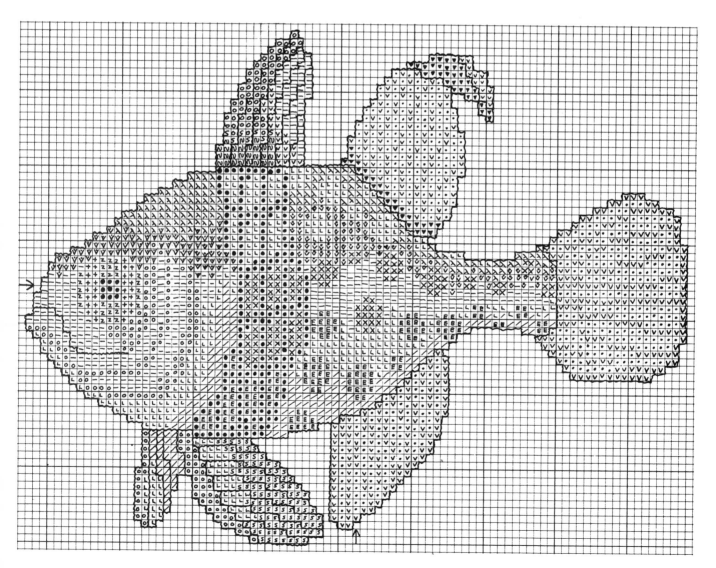

▼ **Bengal Snapper Border**
Lutjanus bengalensis

22-stitch repeat by 24 stitches

BACK-STITCH	CROSS-STITCH	DMC #	
	●	310†	black
	✖	517	dark Wedgwood blue
	L	519*	sky blue
	⧄	747*	very light sky blue
∿∿∿		937	medium avocado green

*Use 1 strand of Balger Blending Filament #094 star blue with each of these colors
†Use 1 strand of Balger Blending Filament #091 star yellow with this color

Imelda's Seaperch ▶
Mirolabrichthys imeldae

51 stitches by 29 stitches

BACK-STITCH	CROSS-STITCH	DMC #	
		300	very dark mahogany
	●	310	black
	L	317	pewter gray
	◣	606	bright orange red
∿∿∿	s	720	dark bittersweet
+++		721	bittersweet

BACK-STITCH	CROSS-STITCH	DMC #	
	▼	722	medium bittersweet
	·	745	light yellow
	I	758	light terra-cotta
	✖	799	medium Delft blue
	⧄	945	medium apricot

▼ **Blue Hamlet**
Hypoplectrus gemma

56 stitches by 29 stitches

BACK-STITCH	CROSS-STITCH	DMC #	
	●	310	black
	⧄	813*	light blue
	▼	825	dark blue
	✖	826*	medium blue
∿∿∿	I	827†	very light blue

*Use 1 strand of Balger Blending Filament #006 blue with each of these colors
†Use 1 strand of Balger Blending Filament #014 sky blue with this color

▼ Oriental Sweetlips
Plectorhinchus orientalis

60 stitches by 28 stitches

	Cross-Stitch	DMC #	
·			white
●		310	black
		414	dark steel gray
⊿		415	pearl gray

Back-Stitch
∿∿

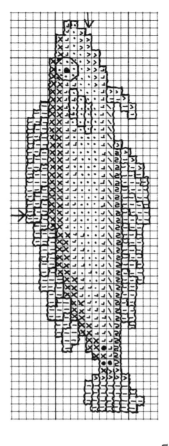

Greenband Wrasse ▲
Halichoeres bathyphilus

52 stitches by 17 stitches

	Cross-Stitch	DMC #	
·			white
●		310	black
⊿		318	light steel gray
L		741	medium tangerine
⊿		762	very light pearl gray
I		772	very light loden green
⊠		891	dark carnation pink
V		3364	light loden green

Back-Stitch
——
∿∿

▼ Whitley's Boxfish
Ostracion whitleyi

44 stitches by 19 stitches

	Cross-Stitch	DMC #	
·			white
●		310	black
I		415	pearl gray
		422	light hazelnut brown
⊿		762	very light pearl gray
◢		918	dark red copper
⊿		920	medium copper
⊿		922	light copper

French Knot
○ ✕

Back-Stitch
|
‒ ‒
∿∿

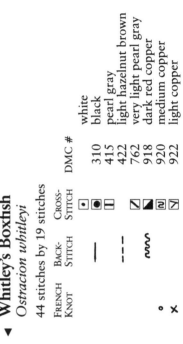

Coolie Loach ▶

Acanthophthalmus kuhli sumatranus

45 stitches by 23 stitches

FRENCH KNOT	BACK-STITCH	CROSS-STITCH	DMC #	
✕	—	▲	300	very dark mahogany
		✕	301	medium mahogany
		₪	400	dark mahogany
		V	720	dark bittersweet
		▯	721	bittersweet
		⁄	722	medium bittersweet

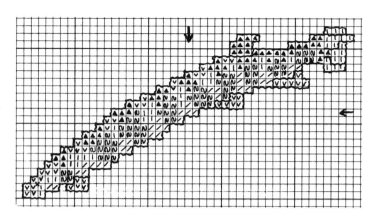

▼ Paradise Fish

Macropodus opercularis

78 stitches by 57 stitches

BACK-STITCH	CROSS-STITCH	DMC #	
	⬤	310	black
	⧄	340	medium lilac
	⧅	341	light lilac
	✕	352	light coral
	♥	353	peach
	⊟	444	dark lemon yellow
	⊞	754	light peach
∿		926	medium gray blue
	₪	3345	dark hunter green
	L	3346	hunter green
	⁄	3347	medium yellow green

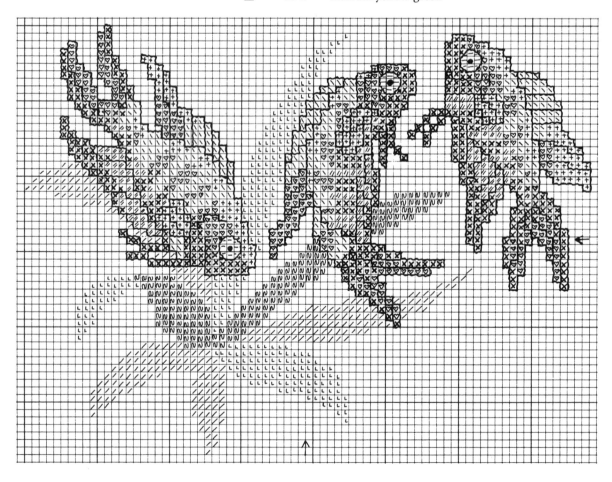

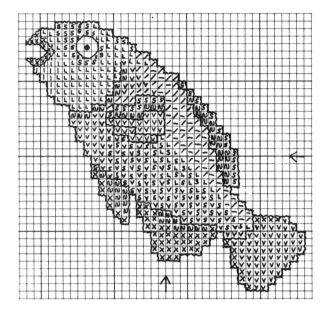

Rusty Parrotfish
Scarus ferrugineus

38 stitches by 36 stitches

BACK-STITCH	CROSS-STITCH	DMC #	
—	◖	310	black
	⋈	420	dark hazelnut brown
	⌷	676	light old gold
	⊟	677	very light old gold
	∇	729	medium old gold
∿∿		911	medium emerald green
	⊠	912*	light emerald green
	⑀	913*	medium Nile green
	⊘	954*	Nile green
	⬚	955*	light Nile green

*Use 1 strand of Balger Blending Filament #008 green with these colors

Siamese Fighting Fish ▶
Betta splendens

33 stitches by 40 stitches

FRENCH KNOT	BACK-STITCH	CROSS-STITCH	DMC #	
		∇	321	Christmas red
		⋈	322	dark marine blue
			336	navy blue
•	—	⊡	775	light baby blue
		▲	816	garnet red
		◣	919	red copper
		⊠	920	medium copper
		⬚	922	light copper
		⊘	3325	baby blue

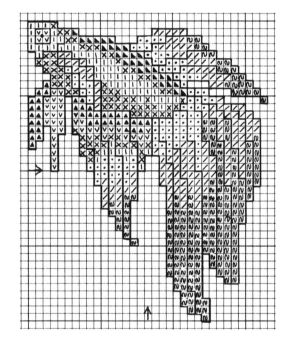

◀ Ornate Butterflyfish
Chaetodon ornatissimus

41 stitches by 33 stitches

FRENCH KNOT	BACK-STITCH	CROSS-STITCH	DMC #	
		⊡		white
•	—	●	310	black
		⊠	921	copper
		⊘	927	light gray blue
		⬚	928	very light gray blue
		⊟	973	bright canary yellow

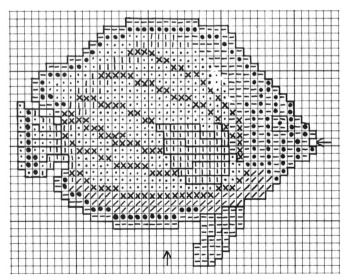

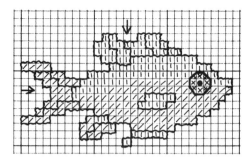

▲ Wagtail Platyfish
Xiphophorus maculatus

29 stitches by 15 stitches

BACK-STITCH	CROSS-STITCH	DMC #	
∿∿		301	medium mahogany
	⦿	310	black
	✕	740	tangerine
	Ⅰ	741	medium tangerine
	⧄	742	light tangerine
	·	743	dark yellow

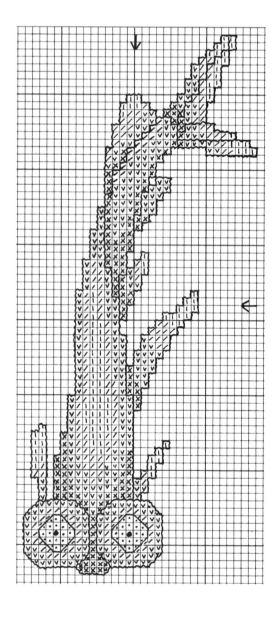

▼ Fourline Wrasse
Larabicus quadrilineatus

41 stitches by 20 stitches

BACK-STITCH	CROSS-STITCH	DMC #	
——	⦿	310	black
	◣	797	royal blue
	ᴎ	995*	dark electric blue
	⧄	996	medium electric blue

*Use 1 strand of Balger Blending Filament #006HL high luster blue with this color

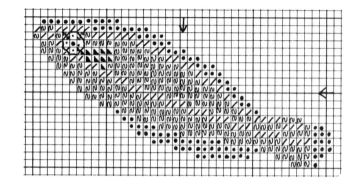

◄ Celestial Telescope Goldfish
Carassius auratus

33 stitches by 72 stitches

BACK-STITCH	CROSS-STITCH	DMC #	
	·		white
——	⦿	310	black
	Ⅰ	402*	very light mahogany
	✕	720*	dark bittersweet
	⩔	721*	bittersweet
	⧄	722*	medium bittersweet
∿∿		919	red copper

*Use 1 strand of Balger Blending Filament #027 orange with each of these colors

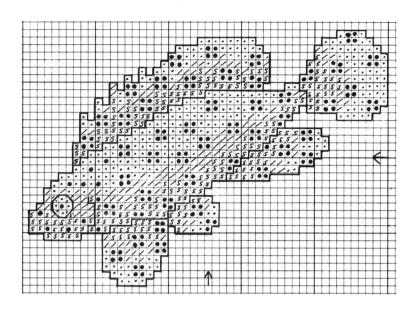

▲ Panther Grouper
Cromileptes altivelis

49 stitches by 34 stitches

BACK-STITCH	CROSS-STITCH	DMC #	
	·	*	white
—	●	310†	black
	S	318^	light steel gray
	⧄	762^	very light pearl gray

*Use 1 strand of Balger Blending Filament #100 white with this color

†Use 1 strand of Balger Blending Filament #005 black with this color

^ Use 1 strand of Balger Blending Filament #032 pearl with these colors

▼ Silver Hatchetfish
Gasteropelecus sternicla

58 stitches by 34 stitches

BACK-STITCH	CROSS-STITCH	DMC #	
	·		white
—	●	310	black
	✳	317	pewter gray
	L	318	light steel gray
	⊓	415	pearl gray
∿∿		701	light Christmas green
	⧄	703	chartreuse

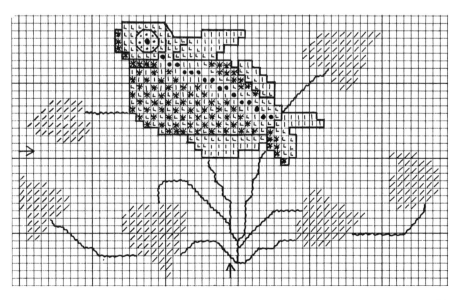

Black Tetra ▶
Gymnocorymbus ternetzi

76 stitches by 47 stitches

BACK-STITCH	CROSS-STITCH	DMC #	
—	●	310	black
	ท	469	avocado green
	L	471	light avocado green
	/	472	very light avocado green
	X	645	very dark beaver gray
	V	647	medium beaver gray
	o	676	light old gold
	S	680	dark old gold
	+	729	medium old gold
	I	747	very light sky blue
	⊟	3024	very light brown gray

▼ New Guinea Red Rainbowfish
Glossalepsis incisus

75 stitches by 71 stitches

BACK-STITCH	CROSS-STITCH	DMC #	
—	•	310	black
∿∿	ท	318	light steel gray
	∥	349	dark coral
	X	351	coral
	−	353	peach
	╱	471	light avocado green
	॥	701	light Christmas green
	╲	702	kelly green
	7	703	chartreuse
	V	905	dark parrot green
	c	907	light parrot green
	◥	937	medium avocado green
	S	975	dark golden brown
	L	976	medium golden brown
	o	977	light golden brown

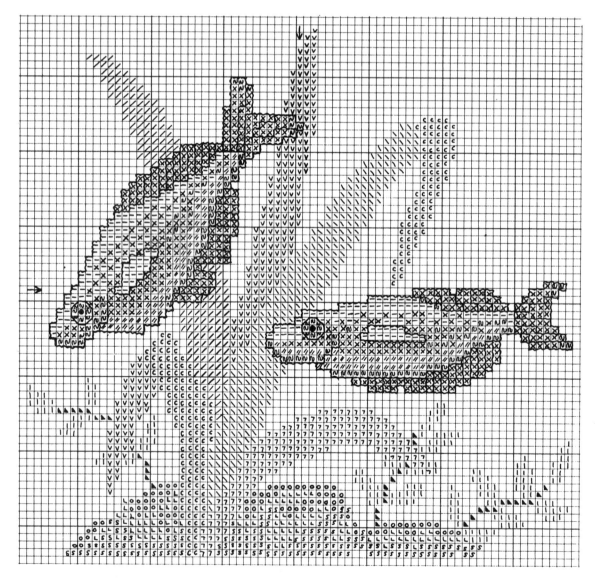

24

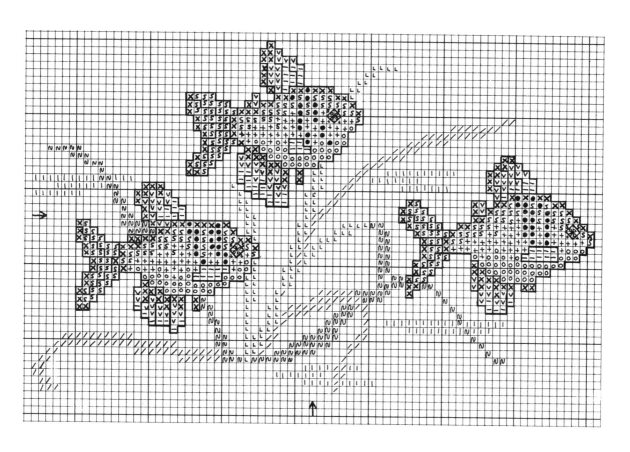

▼ Long-nosed Butterflyfish

Chalmon rostratus

74 stitches by 42 stitches

BACK-STITCH	CROSS-STITCH	DMC #		BACK-STITCH	CROSS-STITCH	DMC #	
	·		white		Ⓝ	720	dark bittersweet
	●	310	black		◣	721	bittersweet
	L	318	light steel gray		Ⅰ	722	medium bittersweet
∾∾		413	dark pewter gray		◿	762	very light pearl gray
	Ц	414	dark steel gray				

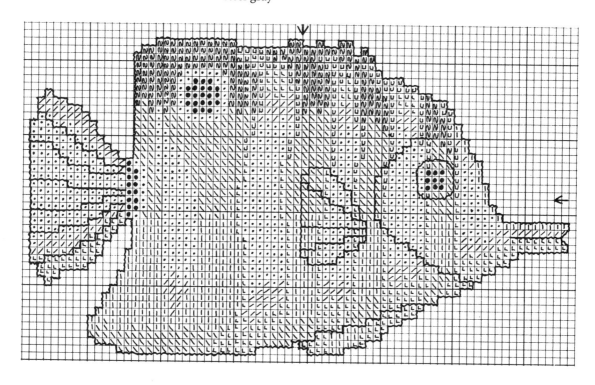

Polkadot Cardinalfish ▶

Sphaeramia nematopterus

32 stitches by 37 stitches

BACK-STITCH	CROSS-STITCH	DMC #	
	⊡		white
——	⬤	310	black
	◪	317	pewter gray
	⊠	318	light steel gray
	⊙	414	dark steel gray
	◹	762	very light pearl gray
	N	832	dark golden wheat
	L	833	medium golden wheat
∿∿	◣	922	light copper

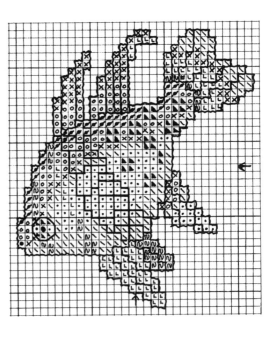

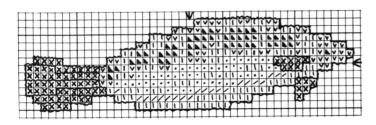

◀ ## Spottail Coris

Coris caudimacula

45 stitches by 12 stitches

BACK-STITCH	CROSS-STITCH	DMC #	
	⊡		white
∿∿	◣	300	very dark mahogany
	⊠	301	medium mahogany
	◪	318	light steel gray
	⊞	721	bittersweet
	V	722	medium bittersweet

Discus Fish ▶

Symphysodon discus

35 stitches by 39 stitches

BACK-STITCH	CROSS-STITCH	DMC #	
	⊡		white
	⬤	310	black
∿∿	⊠	355	very dark terra-cotta
	L	356	dark terra-cotta
- - -	⊙	720	dark bittersweet
	◪	721	bittersweet
	⊞	722	medium bittersweet

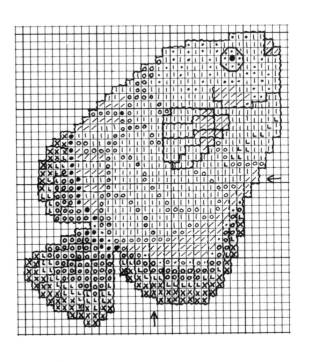

Powder-blue Surgeonfish ▶
Acanthurus leucosternon

40 stitches by 35 stitches

BACK-STITCH	CROSS-STITCH	DMC #	
	⊡		white
—	◙	310	black
∿∿	◤	311	medium navy blue
	N	322	dark marine blue
	S	334	medium marine blue
	╱	772	very light loden green
	⊟	3325	baby blue
	L	3348	light yellow green

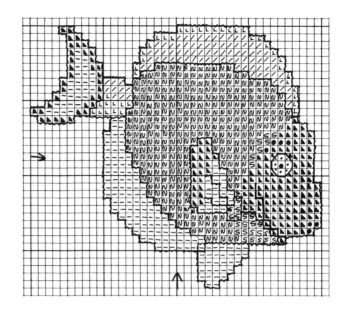

◀ Eightline Wrasse
Paracheilinus octotaenia

48 stitches by 37 stitches

BACK-STITCH	CROSS-STITCH	DMC #	
	◙	310	black
	◤	333	dark lilac
	╱	340	medium lilac
	N	350	medium coral
	◯	352	light coral
	╱	725	topaz
	L	782	medium topaz
	☐	783	Christmas gold
·····	S	792	dark cornflower blue
	⊞	793	medium cornflower blue
	⊟	794	light cornflower blue
∿∿	✳	816	garnet red
	♡	817	very dark coral

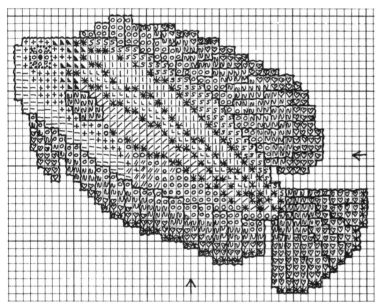

Yellowhead Jawfish ▶
Opisthognathus aurifrons

33 stitches by 35 stitches

BACK-STITCH	CROSS-STITCH	DMC #	
	⊡		white
	⊟	307	lemon yellow
	◙	310	black
	V	444	dark lemon yellow
	I	445	light lemon yellow
∿∿		519	sky blue
	╱	747	very light sky blue

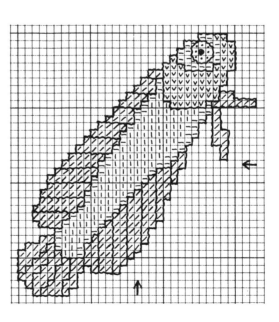

▲ **Clown Coris**
Coris aygula

78 stitches by 37 stitches

Back-Stitch	Cross-Stitch	DMC #	
	·		white
	●	310	black
	◨	740	tangerine
	◿	926	medium gray blue
	⌐	927	light gray blue
	⌐	928	very light gray blue
	⌐	931	medium antique blue
⌁	◨	932	light antique blue
	☒	947	burnt orange

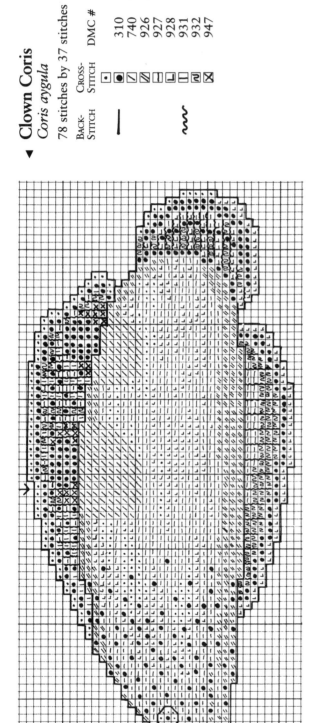

Achilles Tang ▶
Acanthurus achilles

63 stitches by 28 stitches

Back-Stitch	Cross-Stitch	DMC #	
	·		white
	●	310	black
	◨	311	medium navy blue
	⌐	322	dark marine blue
	◿	608	bright orange
	◿	740	tangerine
	☒	823	dark navy blue

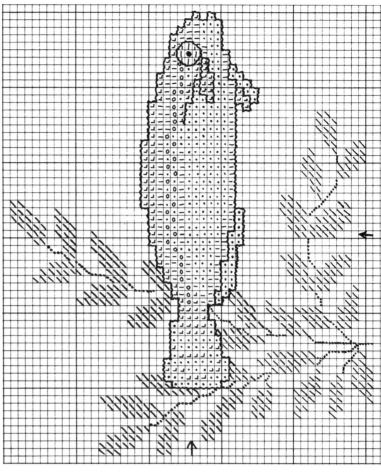

▲ Neon Tetra
Paracheirodon innesi

53 stitches by 49 stitches

BACK-STITCH	CROSS-STITCH	DMC #	
—	●	310	black
	✷	608	bright orange
	◪	702	kelly green
	⊥	704	bright chartreuse
	ℕ	926	medium gray blue
	⊞	927	light gray blue
	◖	928	very light gray blue
	⊏	996	medium electric blue

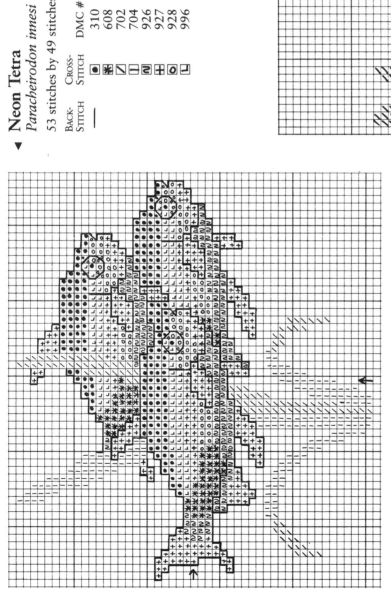

Zigzag Wrasse ▲
Halichoeres scapularis

59 stitches by 50 stitches

BACK-STITCH	CROSS-STITCH	DMC #	
	·	*	white
	●◖	310	black
	⊔	318*	light steel gray
	⊤	415	pearl gray
	Ⅱ	741	medium tangerine
		762*	very light pearl gray
	◪	904	very dark parrot green
∿∿∿	◉	906	medium parrot green
· · · · ·		3608	fuchsia

*Use 1 strand of Balger Blending Filament #032 pearl with these colors

29

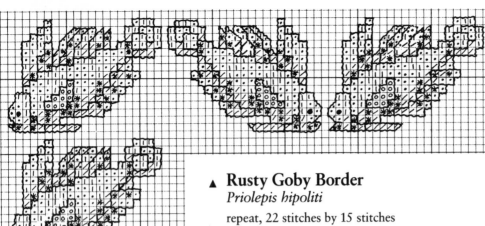

▲ Rusty Goby Border
Priolepis hipoliti

repeat, 22 stitches by 15 stitches

BACK-STITCH	CROSS-STITCH	DMC #	
	·		white
	╱	318	light steel gray
∿	●	415	pearl gray
	✳	740	tangerine
	⊓	741	medium tangerine
	○	743	dark yellow

Blue Damselfish ▶
Pomacentrus coelestis

35 stitches by 23 stitches

FRENCH KNOT	BACK-STITCH	CROSS-STITCH	DMC #	
	—	●	310	black
		⋈	725	topaz
		○	783	Christmas gold
■		Ͷ	995	dark electric blue
		L	996	medium electric blue

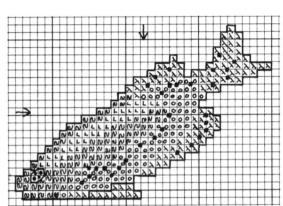

◀ Spotfin Hagfish Corner
Bodianus pulchellus

49 stitches by 49 stitches

BACK-STITCH	CROSS-STITCH	DMC #	
	·		white
—	●	310	black
●–●–●	◢	321	Christmas red
	⊓	415	pearl gray
∿	◺	606	bright orange red
– – –	⊟	741	medium tangerine
	⅃	742	light tangerine

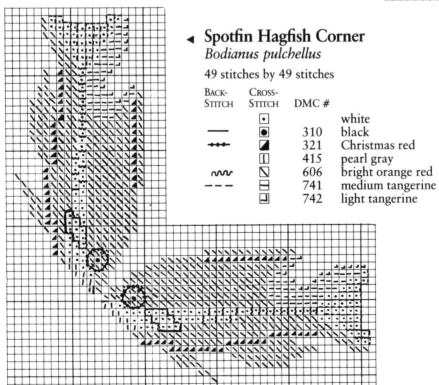

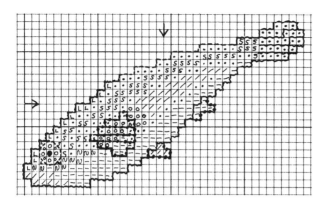

◄ **Threeline Wrasse**
Stethojulis trilineata

38 stitches by 22 stitches

BACK-STITCH	CROSS-STITCH	DMC #	
	⊡	310	black
◄◄◄		518	light Wedgwood blue
	⧄	519	sky blue
	L	522	olive drab
	S	725	topaz
	⊟	747	very light sky blue
∿∿		780	very dark topaz
	N	783	Christmas gold
- - - -		947	burnt orange
	○	972	yellow orange

▼ **Cardinalfish**

67 stitches by 58 stitches

BACK-STITCH	CROSS-STITCH	DMC #		BACK-STITCH	CROSS-STITCH	DMC #	
	⊡		white	·······	⊞	780	very dark topaz
—	●	310	black		V	783	Christmas gold
	⧄	415	pearl gray		7	893	light carnation pink
	N	502	blue green		⧄⧄	894	very light carnation pink
	♥	503	medium blue green		○	3051	dark gray green
∿∿	X	606	bright orange red		⊓	3053	gray green
	⊟	725	topaz				

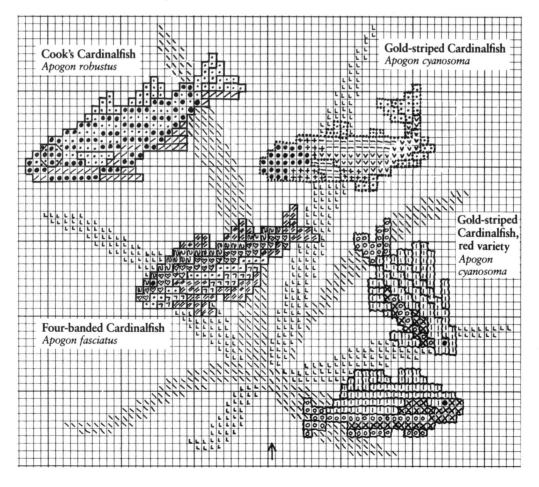

Cook's Cardinalfish
Apogon robustus

Gold-striped Cardinalfish
Apogon cyanosoma

Gold-striped Cardinalfish, red variety
Apogon cyanosoma

Four-banded Cardinalfish
Apogon fasciatus

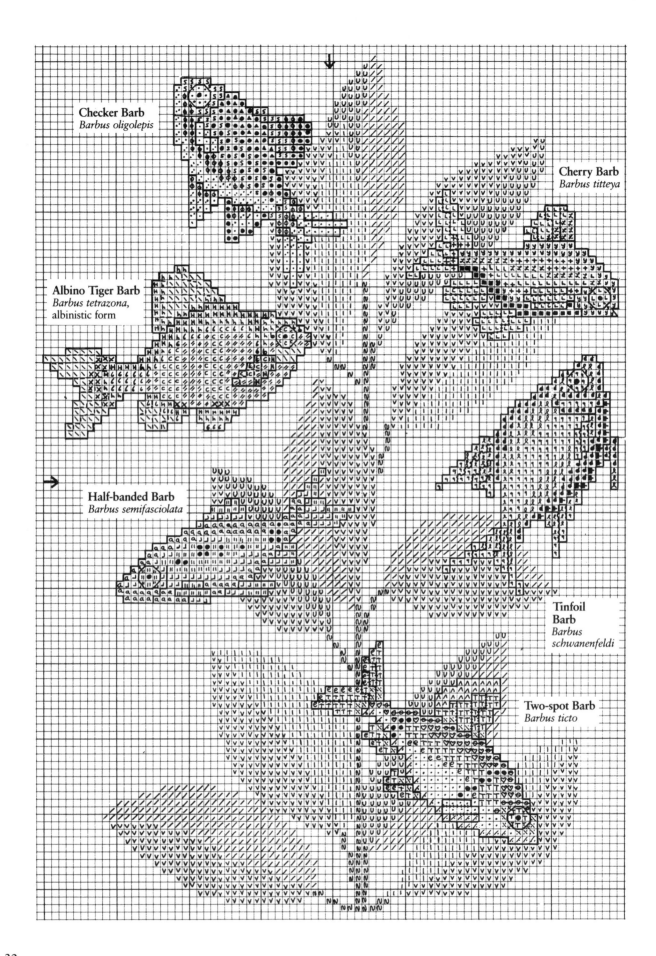

Checker Barb
Barbus oligolepis

Cherry Barb
Barbus titteya

Albino Tiger Barb
Barbus tetrazona,
albinistic form

Half-banded Barb
Barbus semifasciolata

Tinfoil Barb
Barbus schwanenfeldi

Two-spot Barb
Barbus ticto

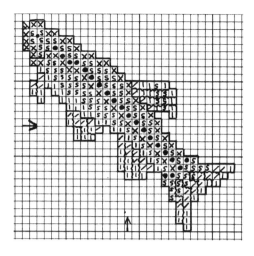

◄ White Cloud Mountain Minnow
Tanichthys albonubes

29 stitches by 28 stitches

FRENCH KNOT	BACK-STITCH	CROSS-STITCH	DMC #	
•		Ⅱ	307	lemon yellow
	—	●	310	black
	∿		413	dark pewter gray
		S	606*	bright orange red
		⁄	608*	bright orange
		✕	666*	bright Christmas red

*Use 1 strand of Balger Blending Filament #208 orange with these colors

◄ Barb Fish

79 stitches by 114 stitches

BACK-STITCH	CROSS-STITCH	DMC #	
	⊡		white
—	◉	310	black
╫		318	light steel gray
	⊖	340	medium lilac
	♡	341	light lilac
	■	349	dark coral
	₩	350	medium coral
	⊞	351	coral
	⌷	352	light coral
✦✦✦	✕	414	dark steel gray
	⁄	415	pearl gray
∿	⊞	420	dark hazelnut brown
	Ⅵ	469	avocado green
	⁄	470	medium light avocado green
	Ⅴ	471	light avocado green
	Ⅱ	472	very light avocado green
	Ⅱ	580	dark moss green
	⋀	608	bright orange
	▲	640	dark beige gray
	S	642	medium beige gray
	Φ	644	light beige gray
	⊓	676	light old gold
	⌐	680	dark old gold
	☒	729	medium old gold
	⌠	740	tangerine
	⁄	742	light tangerine
	Ⅱ	743	dark yellow
	✕	744	medium yellow
	⌂	745	light yellow
	Ⅱ	760	salmon
	⊤	761	light salmon
	℮	818	baby pink
	⊡	822	light beige gray
- - -	⊟	946	medium burnt orange
	⊟	947	burnt orange
	⊡	975	dark golden brown
	⌐	976	medium golden brown
	Ⅱ	977	light golden brown

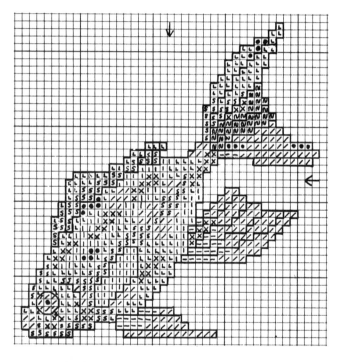

▲ Shubunkin Goldfish
Carassius auratus

41 stitches by 42 stitches

BACK-STITCH	CROSS-STITCH	DMC #	
—	●	310	black
	✕	666	bright Christmas red
	⊞	741	medium tangerine
	⁄	743	dark yellow
	S	813*	light blue
	L	826*	medium blue
	Ⅰ	827*	very light blue
	Ⅵ	907	light parrot green

*Use 1 strand of Balger Blending Filament #014 sky blue with each of these colors

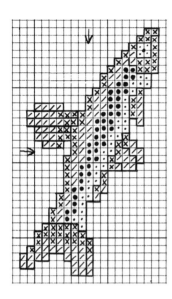
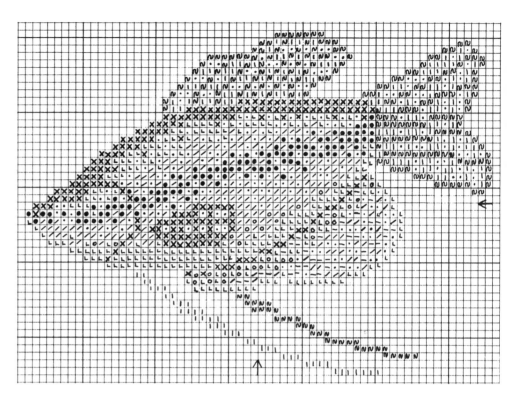

▲ Golden Pencilfish
Nannostomus beckfordi

19 stitches by 33 stitches

French Knot	Back-Stitch	Cross-Stitch	DMC #	
•	—	●	310	black
		✖	725	topaz
		⧄	726	light topaz
		⊡	727	very light topaz

▼ Pencilfish
Nannostomus

51 stitches by 18 stitches

Back-Stitch	Cross-Stitch	DMC #	
	⊡		white
—	●	310	black
	⌊	334	medium marine blue
	⊙	444	dark lemon yellow
	✖	606	bright orange red
	⊟	608	bright orange
	⧄	775	light baby blue

▲ Pearl or Lace Gourami
Trichogaster leeri

64 stitches by 46 stitches

	DMC #	
⊡		white
●	310	black
ℕ	400	dark mahogany
⊙	415	pearl gray
⌊	606*	bright orange red
⧄	608*	bright orange
✖	666*	bright Christmas red
⊟	740*	tangerine
Ⅱ	921	copper

*Use 1 strand of Balger's Blending Filament #003 red with these colors

Underwater Scene

81 stitches by 71 stitches

BACK-STITCH	CROSS-STITCH	DMC #	
	•		white
┼┼┼┼	▼	210	medium lavender
	●	310	black
	6	318	light steel gray
	∠	340	medium lilac
	C	341	light lilac
	■	413	dark pewter gray
┼•┼•┼	Z	414	dark steel gray
	Λ	415	pearl gray
	L	470	medium light avocado green
	V	471	light avocado green
	/	472	very light avocado green
	∾	518	light Wedgwood blue
	Ⅲ	519	sky blue

BACK-STITCH	CROSS-STITCH	DMC #	
	S	522	olive drab
	I	524	light olive drab
	e	702	kelly green
	U	704	bright chartreuse
	⊡	762	very light pearl gray
- - -		937	medium avocado green
	⌐	945	medium apricot
•◆•◆•		991	dark aquamarine
	Φ	993	light aquamarine
	X	3608	fuchsia
	⊘	3609	light fuchsia
	J	3705	watermelon
	◀	3708	light watermelon

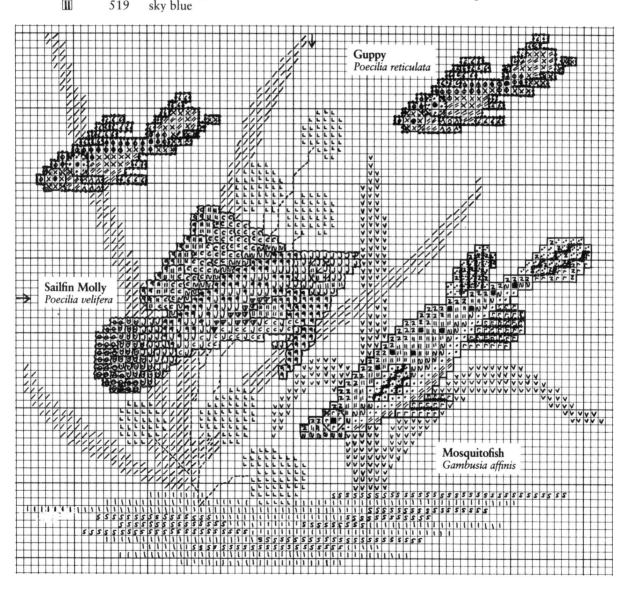

35

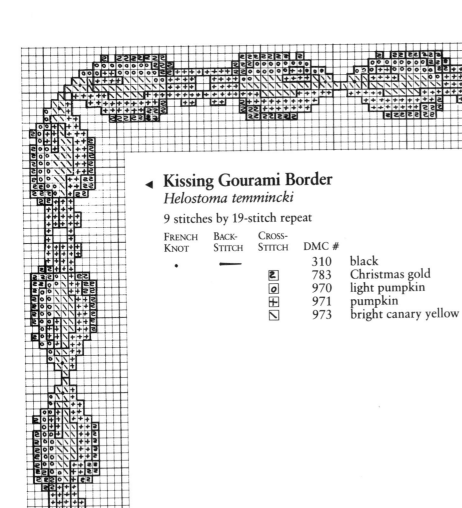

◄ Kissing Gourami Border
Helostoma temmincki

9 stitches by 19-stitch repeat

FRENCH KNOT	BACK-STITCH	CROSS-STITCH	DMC #	
•	—		310	black
		Ƨ	783	Christmas gold
		o	970	light pumpkin
		+	971	pumpkin
		⊠	973	bright canary yellow

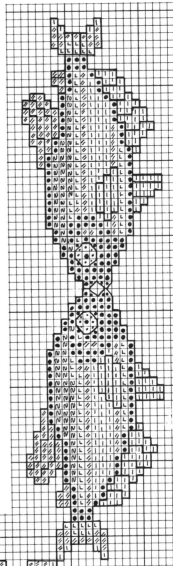

Silver Tetra Border ►
Ctenobrycon spilurus

36-stitch repeat by 19 stitches

BACK-STITCH	CROSS-STITCH	DMC #	
	•		white
—	●	310	black
	L	317	pewter gray
	⁄⁄	318	light steel gray
	ℕ	413	dark pewter gray
	∏	415	pearl gray

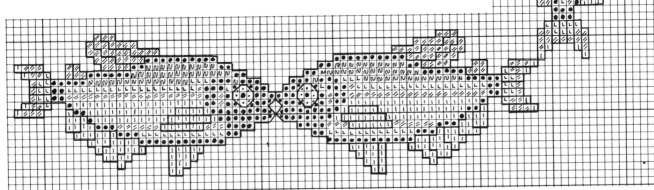

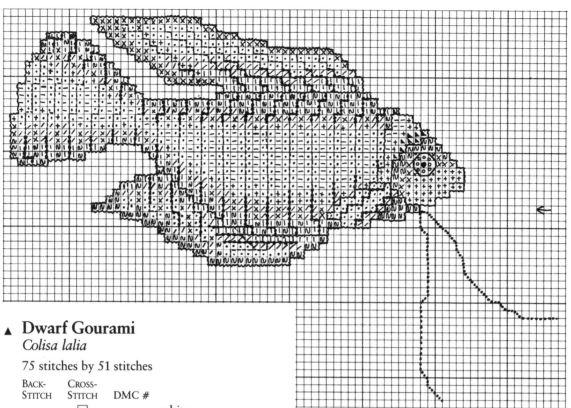

▲ Dwarf Gourami
Colisa lalia

75 stitches by 51 stitches

BACK-STITCH	CROSS-STITCH	DMC #	
	·		white
——	●	310	black
	⊥	318	light steel gray
······	☒	321	Christmas red
∿∿		517	dark Wedgwood blue
– – –		518	light Wedgwood blue
◆◆◆	◣	519	sky blue
	⊞	606	bright orange red
	⊟	608	bright orange
	∕	762	very light pearl gray
	͈	816	garnet red
	⊙	973	bright canary yellow

Firemouth Cichlid ▶
Cichlasoma meeki

37 stitches by 41 stitches

BACK-STITCH	CROSS-STITCH	DMC #	
	·		white
——	●	310	black
	⊥	318	light steel gray
	S	350	medium coral
	⊟	351	coral
	͈	414	dark steel gray
	∕	415	pearl gray
∿∿	☒	817	very dark coral

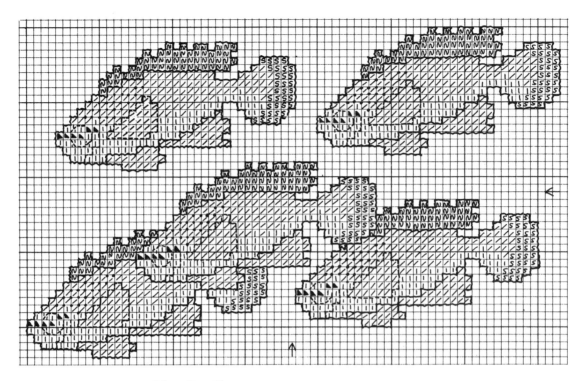

▲ **Blue Devil**
Chrysiptera cyanea

73 stitches by 44 stitches

FRENCH KNOT	BACK-STITCH	CROSS-STITCH	DMC #	
•	- - - -		517	dark Wedgwood blue
		Ⴖ	518	light Wedgwood blue
		Ⅱ	519	sky blue
		S	721	bittersweet
		∕	747	very light sky blue
∿∿∿		◣	796	dark royal blue

▼ **Clown Loach**
Botia macracantha

40 stitches by 20 stitches

BACK-STITCH	CROSS-STITCH	DMC #	
——	⊙	310	black
	∕	352	light coral
	⊠	606	bright orange red
	Ⅴ	3047	light yellow beige
	Ⅱ	3078	very light golden yellow

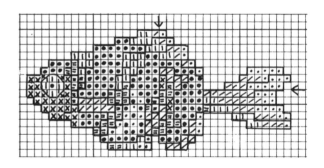

▲ **Black Ruby Barb**
Barbus nigrofasciatus

36 stitches by 16 stitches

BACK-STITCH	CROSS-STITCH	DMC #	
——	⊙	310	black
	☰	740	tangerine
	Ⅱ	741	medium tangerine
	∕	742	light tangerine
	•	743	dark yellow
	⊠	947	burnt orange

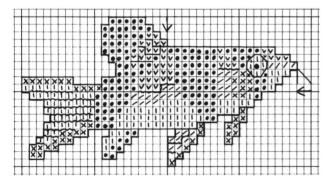

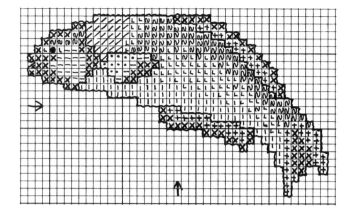

◄ Cortez Rainbow Wrasse
Thalassoma lucasanum

41 stitches by 24 stitches

BACK-STITCH	CROSS-STITCH	DMC #	
	·		white
	●	310	black
	Ͷ	335	rose
	⊞	798	dark Delft blue
	ʟ	899	medium rose
	⁄	973	bright canary yellow
~~	☒	995	dark electric blue
	⊟	996	medium electric blue
	⊡	3326	light rose

Orange-tipped Rainbowfish ►
Halichoeres melanurus

28 stitches by 31 stitches

BACK-STITCH	CROSS-STITCH	DMC #	
—	●	310	black
	⁄	813	light blue
	Ͷ	825	dark blue
	⊞	826	medium blue
	ʟ	912	light emerald green
	o	947	burnt orange
	⊡	954	Nile green

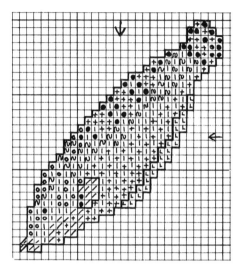

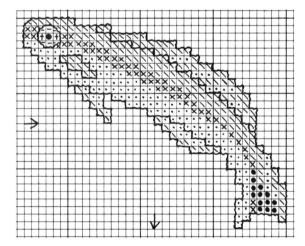

▲ Redstripe Tilefish
Hoplolatilus marcosi

28 stitches by 36 stitches

BACK-STITCH	CROSS-STITCH	DMC #	
	·	*	white
	●	310	black
~~	⊞	318	light steel gray
	◲	352†	light coral
	☒	606#	bright orange red
	⊟	996	medium electric blue

*Use 1 strand of Balger Blending Filament #100
white with this color

†Use 1 strand of Balger Blending Filament #007
pink with this color

#Use 1 strand of Balger Blending Filament #003
red with this color

▼ Squirrelfish
Holocentrus

20 stitches by 21 stitches

BACK-STITCH	CROSS-STITCH	DMC #	
	⊟	402	very light mahogany
	☒	720	dark bittersweet
	⁄	721	bittersweet
	⊡	722	medium bittersweet
~~	▲	938	ultra dark coffee brown

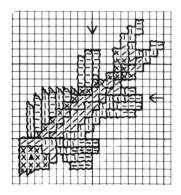

Lyretail Coralfish ▶

Pseudanthias squamipinnis

48 stitches by 28 stitches

BACK-STITCH	CROSS-STITCH	DMC #	
	M	340	medium lilac
	N	341	light lilac
	⊞	519	sky blue
	Ⅱ	554	light violet
	⊘	747	very light sky blue
∼∼	◼	796	dark royal blue
	⊟	945	medium apricot
	U	977	light golden brown
	▲	995	dark electric blue
	✕	3041	medium antique violet
	N	3687	mauve
	L	3688	medium light mauve

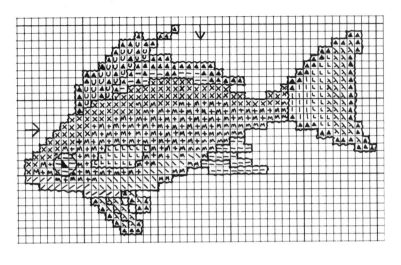

▼ Lyretail Swordtail

Xiphophorus helleri

85 stitches by 49 stitches

FRENCH KNOT	BACK-STITCH	CROSS-STITCH	DMC #	
✕	∼∼		300	very dark mahogany
		⊠	608	bright orange
		⋁	720	dark bittersweet
		⊟	721	bittersweet
		L	722	medium bittersweet
		o	742	light tangerine
		S	833	medium golden wheat
		N	919	red copper
		✕	921	copper
		⊘	3347	medium yellow green
		Ⅱ	3348	light yellow green

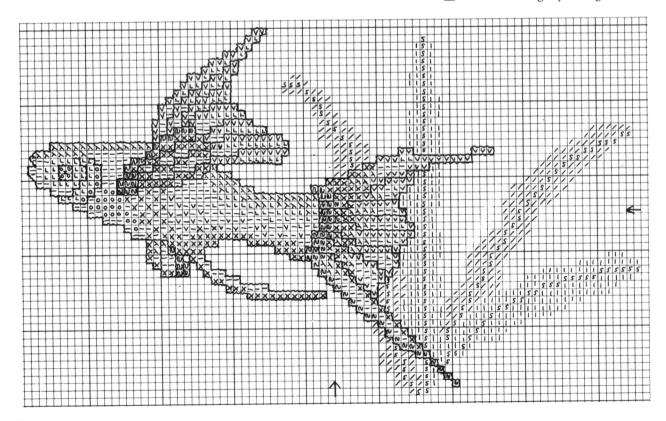

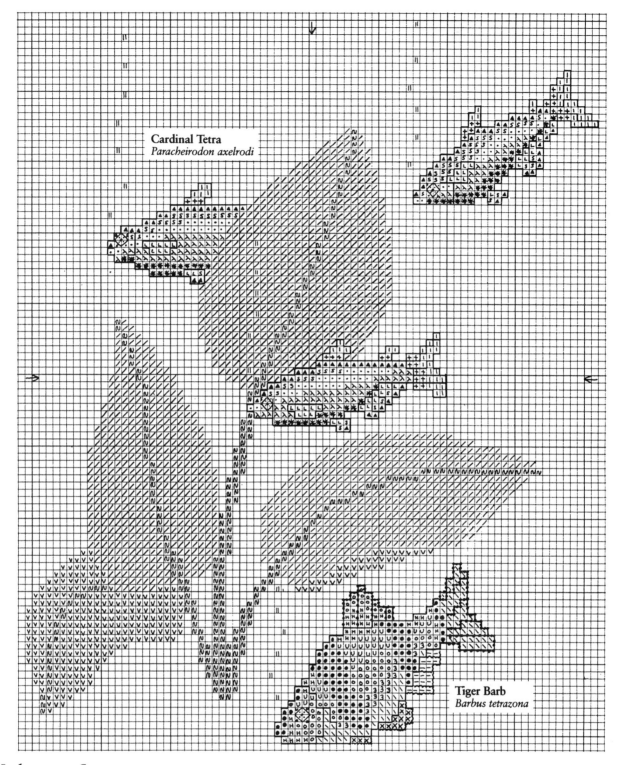

Cardinal Tetra
Paracheirodon axelrodi

Tiger Barb
Barbus tetrazona

Underwater Scene

83 stitches by 101 stitches

FRENCH KNOT	BACK-STITCH	CROSS-STITCH	DMC #	
		⊡		white
•	—	◉	310	black
		✱	347	dark salmon
		⊟	452	medium shell gray
		◩	504	light blue green
		▲	517	dark Wedgwood blue
		S	518	light Wedgwood blue
		L	519	sky blue
		V	580	dark moss green
		⁄	581	moss green
		⊠	606	bright orange red

FRENCH KNOT	BACK-STITCH	CROSS-STITCH	DMC #	
		3	608	bright orange
ᔕᔕ			666	bright Christmas red
		I	725	topaz
		＋	783	Christmas gold
		II	828	very pale blue
	•◆•◆•	H	924	very dark gray blue
		U	926	medium gray blue
		O	927	light gray blue
		ℕ	937	medium avocado green
		⋈	3328	medium dark salmon

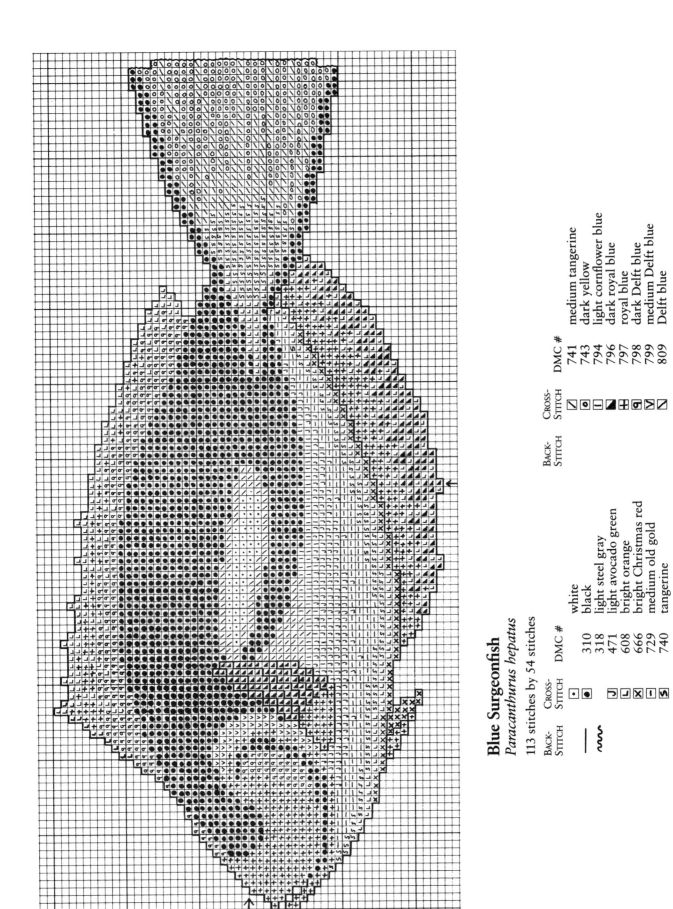

Blue Surgeonfish
Paracanthurus hepatus

113 stitches by 54 stitches

BACK-STITCH	CROSS-STITCH		DMC #	
·	●			white
			310	black
			318	light steel gray
⌐	⌐		471	light avocado green
∟	∟		608	bright orange
✕	✕		666	bright Christmas red
	/		729	medium old gold
	S		740	tangerine

BACK-STITCH	CROSS-STITCH		DMC #	
	⟋		741	medium tangerine
	⊙		743	dark yellow
	⊏		794	light cornflower blue
	◢		796	dark royal blue
	⊞		797	dark royal blue
	◖		798	dark Delft blue
	∨		799	medium Delft blue
	⟍		809	Delft blue

42

▲ **Oualan Forktail Blenny**
Meiacanthus oualanensis
70 stitches by 52 stitches

	CROSS-STITCH	DMC #	
●		301	medium mahogany
∨		310	black
⁄		320	medium pistachio green
✳		368	light pistachio green
◢		610	very dark drab brown
✕		645	very dark beaver gray
∟		646	dark beaver gray
○		648	light beaver gray
│		742	light tangerine
⁄		743	dark yellow
2		744	medium yellow
I		3032	medium mocha brown
		3033	very light mocha brown

BACK-STITCH 〜〜

Emperor Snapper ▶
Lutjanus sebae
62 stitches by 29 stitches

	CROSS-STITCH	DMC #	
●			white
●		310	black
∟		317	pewter gray
⁄		318	light steel gray
⁄		762	very light pearl gray
I		900	dark burnt orange
		947	burnt orange

BACK-STITCH ── 〜〜

43

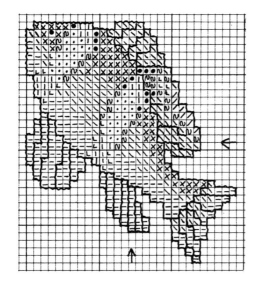

◄ Two-banded Anemonefish
Amphiprion bicinctus

29 stitches by 32 stitches

BACK-STITCH	CROSS-STITCH	DMC #	
	⊡		white
	⬤	310	black
	L	318	light steel gray
	N	414	dark steel gray
	⧄	415	pearl gray
	◩	725	topaz
	⊟	726	light topaz
	⊞	762	very light pearl gray
∿		782	medium topaz
	⊠	783	Christmas gold

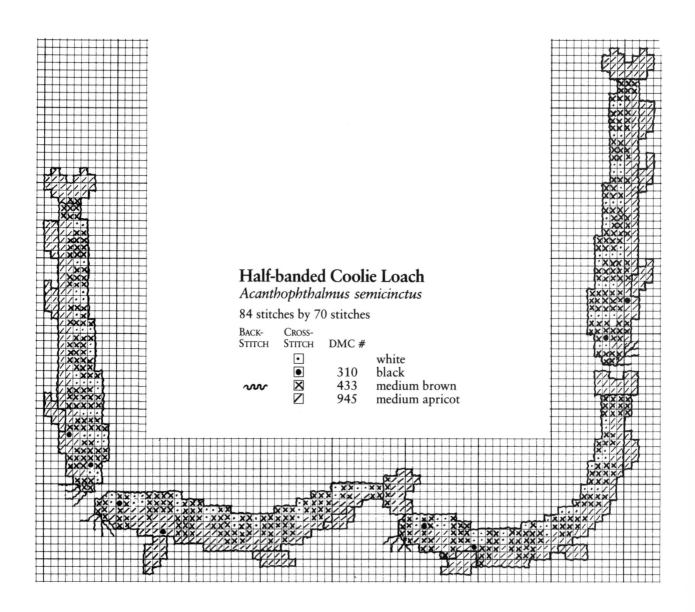

Half-banded Coolie Loach
Acanthophthalmus semicinctus

84 stitches by 70 stitches

BACK-STITCH	CROSS-STITCH	DMC #	
	⊡		white
	⬤	310	black
∿	⊠	433	medium brown
	⧄	945	medium apricot

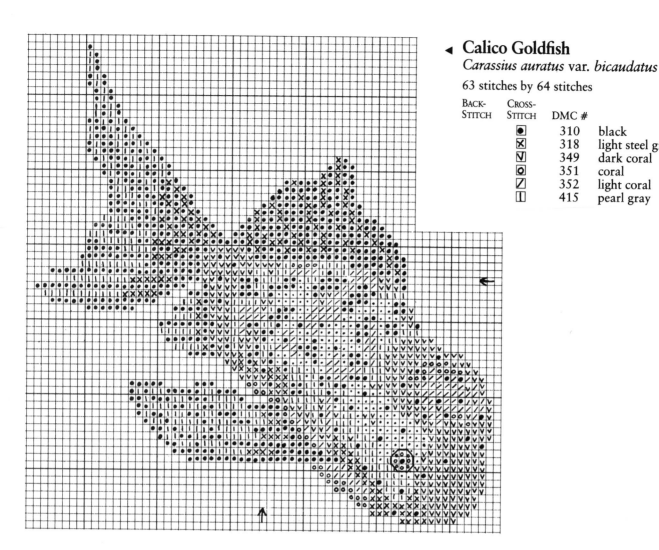

◄ **Calico Goldfish**
Carassius auratus var. *bicaudatus*

63 stitches by 64 stitches

BACK-STITCH	CROSS-STITCH	DMC #	
	⊡	310	black
	☒	318	light steel gray
	Ⅴ	349	dark coral
	⊙	351	coral
	╱	352	light coral
	Ⅱ	415	pearl gray

▼ **Flag Rockfish**
Sebastes rubrovinctus

77 stitches by 28 stitches

BACK-STITCH	CROSS-STITCH	DMC #		BACK-STITCH	CROSS-STITCH	DMC #	
	⊡		white		☒	919	red copper
—	⬤	310	black		Ⅳ	920	medium copper
	⊙	318	light steel gray		Ⅱ	921	copper
	╱	762	very light pearl gray		Ⅴ	922	light copper

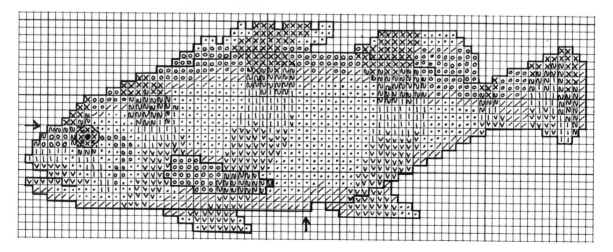

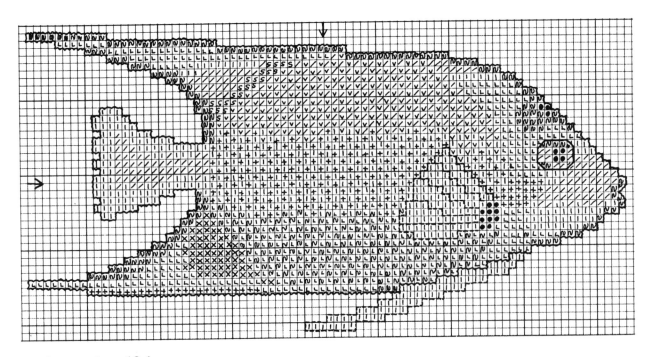

▲ Queen Angelfish
Holocanthus ciliaris

82 stitches by 40 stitches

BACK-STITCH	CROSS-STITCH	DMC #	
——	⊡	310	black
– – –		740	tangerine
	L	742	light tangerine
	I	743	dark yellow
	/	744	medium yellow
∿	N	798	dark Delft blue
	H	799	medium Delft blue
	V	809	Delft blue
	X	992	aquamarine
	S	993	light aquamarine

▼ Red Wagtail Swordtail
Xiphophorus helleri

67 stitches by 26 stitches

BACK-STITCH	CROSS-STITCH	DMC #	
	⊡		white
——	⊙	310	black
	I	606	bright orange red
	V	666	bright Christmas red
	/	741	medium tangerine
	O	743	dark yellow
	X	816	garnet red

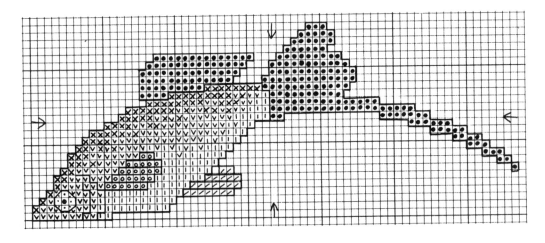

46

Angelfish

Pterophyllum scalare

77 stitches by 101 stitches

BACK-STITCH	CROSS-STITCH	DMC #			BACK-STITCH	CROSS-STITCH	DMC #	
	•		white			☒	413	dark pewter gray
—	◉	310	black			☑	414	dark steel gray
	∿	317	pewter gray			╱	415	pearl gray
	Ⅱ	318	light steel gray			◎	666	bright Christmas red

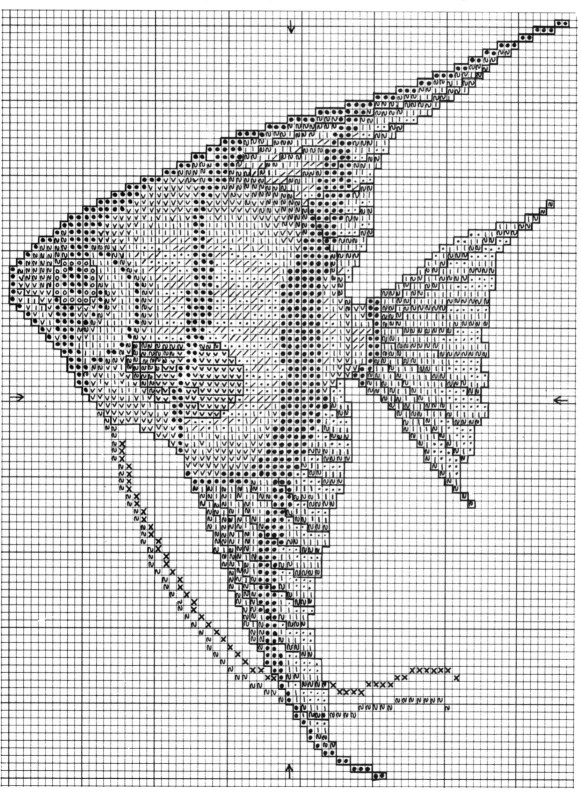

Zebra Danio ▶
Brachydanio rerio

38 stitches by 47 stitches

FRENCH KNOT	BACK-STITCH	CROSS-STITCH	DMC #	
•	—	●	310	black
		S	518	light Wedgwood blue
		V	606	bright orange red
		I	725	topaz
		O	726	light topaz
		•	727	very light topaz
		⊟	747	very light sky blue
		N	975	dark golden brown
		X	976	medium golden brown

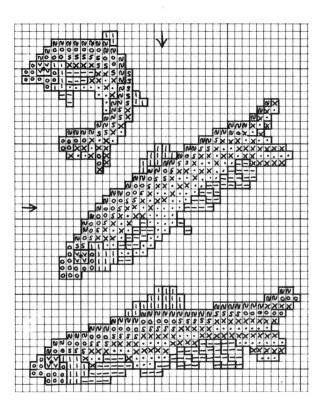

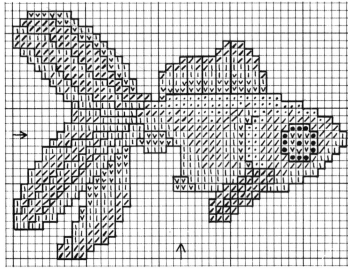

◀ Goldfish
Carassius auratus

46 stitches by 33 stitches

BACK-STITCH	CROSS-STITCH	DMC #	
	I	740	tangerine
	⁄	742	light tangerine
	•	743	dark yellow
	●	919	red copper
—	V	947	burnt orange

Scat ▶
Scatophagus argus

40 stitches by 29 stitches

BACK-STITCH	CROSS-STITCH	DMC #	
	•		white
	●	310	black
	S	924*	very dark gray blue
	X	926*	medium gray blue
	I	927*	light gray blue
	⁄	928*	very light gray blue

*Use 1 strand of Balger Blending Filament #001 silver with these colors

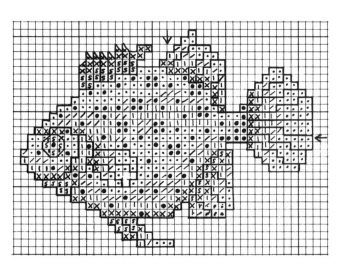